THE UNITED STATES
ARMED FORCES
TODAY

THE UNITED STATES
ARMED FORCES
TODAY

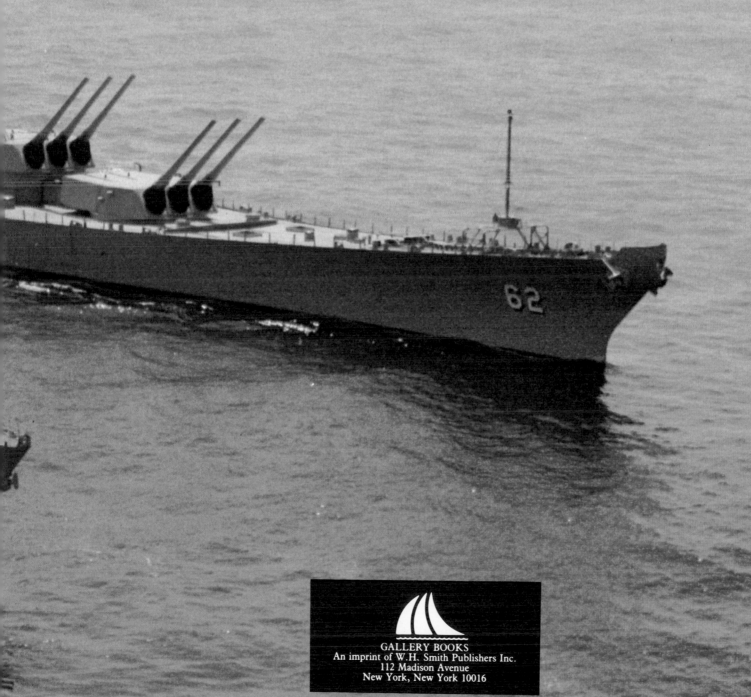

62

GALLERY BOOKS
An imprint of W.H. Smith Publishers Inc.
112 Madison Avenue
New York, New York 10016

Published by Gallery Books
A Division of W H Smith Publishers, Inc
112 Madison Avenue
New York, New York 10016

Produced by
Brompton Books Corp
15 Sherwood Place
Greenwich, CT 06830

ISBN 0-8317-9081-4

Printed in Hong Kong

10 9 8 7 6 5 4 3 2 1

Page 1: A faceless fighter pilot performing smooth maneuvers in his super responsive F-15. Two more Eagles can be seen in formation through the high-visibility cockpit. Photo by George Hall.

Pages 2 – 3: The refurbished US Navy battleship USS *New Jersey* cruises with an escort, the destroyer USS *Fife*. The *New Jersey's* nine 16-inch guns lob projectiles that weigh one ton each.

These pages: There's nothing quite like a full equipment hike when the sun is low in the sky. That's what these US Army soldiers are doing, at the US Army base at Fort Campbell, on the Kentucky/Tennessee border.

Pages 8 – 9: Soldiers of the 82d Airborne Division gather around the flag during a pause in the action in Grenada in 1983.

CONTENTS

Introduction to the United States Army 11
Organization and Structure 25
Weapons of the United States Army 45
Training and Education — The Good Get Better 61
The United States Army in Action 85
Introduction to the United States Navy 107
The Fleet of the United States Navy 125
The United States Navy in Action 185
Introduction to the United States Marines 203
Becoming a United States Marine 221
United States Marines in Action 243
Armed and Equipped to Fight 265
In the Air, on Land and Sea 287
Introduction to the United States Air Force Today 299
The United States Air Force Major Commands 311
Joining the People in Air Force Blue 379
Index 389

THE
US ARMY
TODAY

THE US ARMY TODAY

DA LEVENSON

INTRODUCTION TO THE UNITED STATES ARMY

In a complex and ever-changing world, the US Army is also changing. Today the Army is conducting the most extensive peacetime transition of its 200-year history. Integrated, forward-looking programs are underway, focused on improving organization and doctrine as well as equipping, manning and training troops. The goal: maximum power and the maximum use of that power.

Facing threats ranging from terrorist acts to strategic nuclear war, the Army must be flexible as well as strong. With an active troop force of 780,000 (compared to a Soviet army of three million), the US Army would be outnumbered in the event of a major-power conflict. Since the US forces will never equal those of their most dangerous potential foe, the decision was made in 1984 to maintain the present strength and concentrate on maximizing its use by reorganizing troops and modernizing weapons.

Opposite: **Infantrymen aim their M16s. The upgraded M16A2 is replacing the M16A1 as the Army's standard rifle.**

Right: **Recruits march and shout their 'jody calls' during basic training.**

A major obstacle to combat readiness is the extensive amounts of time and equipment it takes to deploy combat units overseas. To meet this challenge, the Army is restructuring combat divisions for more ready deployment and optimum use of weaponry. Light infantry divisions are being created — divisions with fewer troops and weapons that can be more rapidly deployed anywhere in the world. New weapons systems are modernizing the armor and mechanized divisions; these divisions are being restructured to accommodate systems such as the M1 Abrams tanks, the Bradley Fighting Vehicles and the Multiple Launch Rocket System. In addition, the Army is increasing its reliance on the reserve component forces — the Army Reserve and Army National Guard — and improving their equipment and combat readiness.

The basis for this comprehensive restructuring is the AirLand Battle Doctrine, the Army's blueprint for warfare that combines air and land power for maximum effectiveness. The spectrum of possible warfare runs from terrorism (the lowest level) to all-out nuclear war (highest level). Within the condi-

tion of nuclear stalemate, it is most likely that the US would become involved in a mid-level, or conventional, war if an armed conflict between major powers occurred. The AirLand Battle Doctrine provides a new, nonlinear approach to conventional warfare — one that would give 'leverage' to outnumbered US troops. New strategies, combat units and equipment are being developed to fight the increasing incidence of terrorism and low-intensity conflict.

As defense requirements change, so do training and recruiting requirements. Today, potential soldiers and officers must be better qualified than ever to gain admittance to the Army;

Opposite: **A camouflaged Ranger hones his skills during tactical exercise.**

Top: **Soldiers are briefed prior to 'battle' at the National Training Center.**

Below: **Soldiers depart an M2 Bradley Fighting Vehicle, operational since 1984.**

once in, they must continually improve to remain. Enhanced training and education programs ensure that the good get better. Combat training keeps pace with constantly evolving strategies and weapons systems, adding simulated combat exercises to standard field training.

Throughout this ambitious transition, the Army's 200-year-old mission remains the same — to deter aggression against the United States and her interests, and to fight and win if deterrence fails.

A BRIEF HISTORY

More than 200 years ago, the United States Army began as the Continental Army, formed by the Continental Congress on 14 June 1775 as a revolutionary force against England. Commanded by General George Washington, the new Army consisted of 10 rifle companies and the militias, which were volunteer,

part-time troops lent to Congress by the individual colonies. Many of the militiamen had fought in the French and Indian War of 1763, where they learned the guerilla-style battle techniques of the Indians. This was a prime factor in the Continental Army's victory over the British, who maintained their regimented, European combat style. More than 20,000 American soldiers served in the Revolutionary War.

Immediately following the Revolutionary War, only a few militia units remained intact to guard military supplies at West Point and Fort Pitt. Most of the regular troops were discharged, but the need for ready federal troops became obvious in 1785. The federal government had to borrow state troops to squelch the Whiskey Rebellion in western Pennsylvania and had to step in when state militias could not control Indian uprisings in Ohio, Indiana and Michigan. Congress established a new regular Army, an infantry regiment of 700, supplemented by state troops that came under federal control in wartime. In 1789 Congress established the War Department to direct military activity.

During the War of 1812, the regular Army, with a peak strength of 33,000

Left: **A soldier checks his parachute during airborne training. The three-week airborne course is a physical and mental challenge that prepares paratroopers for the ultimate — the jump *(below)*.**

troops, was greatly outnumbered by the British. The states raised a temporary militia of 100,000 men, but most were poorly trained and many refused to cross the border into Canada in one of the major strategies of the war. However, the regular Army fought well and valiantly. Peace came when the British realized that in unsettled territory such as North America fighting could go on forever with neither side victorious. The postwar Army totaled 10,000 and was used to fight the Indians, who were revolting against the American takeover of their homelands. This Army fought two wars against the Seminole Indians in Florida and the Black Hawk Wars against the Sauk and Fox Indians in Illinois. The Army was also used to force the Cherokee to move to lands west of the Mississippi River, which at the time were considered undesirable by white settlers. The Regiment of Dragoons, forefather of today's 1st Cavalry, was formed in 1833, when the slow-moving infantry proved to be no match for the swift Indian warriors on horseback.

The borders of the young nation were pushed to the Pacific during the Mexican War (1846-48), when steam vessels were used to transport troops

Right and below: **Tank crew members from the 2d Infantry Division during 'Team Spirit 84'; and Army and Air Force personnel working shoulder-to-shoulder during 'Reforger 84' exercises in Europe.**

Army troops convene during a break in the action of 'Reforger' exercises in Germany. NATO conducts annual exercises in areas of Europe most likely to be strategic in the event of a conflict with Warsaw Pact nations.

beyond the US frontier. The regular Army was expanded to a peak strength of 115,000 during the war, but most regiments were disbanded after peace was established, and the Union Army entered the Civil War in 1861 with a mere 16,000 men. However, the Enrollment Act of 1863 instituted the draft, and the Union Army eventually reached a total strength of nearly one million.

The use of railroads, steam engines, and the telegraph, along with the improved range and accuracy of firearms, were major factors in the outcome of the Civil War. Soldiers fought in the unconventional, loose format acquired from the Indians but now strengthened by precision arms and improved transportation and communications systems. The nonindustrialized South was at a serious disadvantage and had tremendous difficulties arming, clothing and feeding its men. The Confederate Army, established by the Confederate Provisional Congress in 1861, reached a peak strength of 900,000 but casualties, disease, capture and desertion left only 174,223 to surrender in 1865.

Relentless war with the Indians throughout America continued until the remaining tribes just ceased to fight. The major campaigns were the Sioux Wars (1854-1890) in the northern plains (where Lieutenant Colonel George Custer made his legendary last stand against Sitting Bull) and the Apache Wars (1861-1900) in the Southwest.

In 1898, the United States Army entered the Spanish-American War with a small force of 28,000, which was doubled during the war and aided by 100,000 National Guardsmen and 125,000 volunteers. The Army was unorganized and ill prepared for battle under the tropical conditions found in Cuba and the Philippine Islands. As a result, a postwar reorganization took place in the early 1900s. The general staff system was established, as was the position of chief of staff.

With World War I came changes in

Both pages: **Scenes from 'Reforger 84,' a NATO exercise held in Europe. A CH-53 helicopter from Semback Air Base, Germany** *(opposite);* **USAF C-130, carrying Army troops, is marshaled into the parking area at RAF Wildenroth, Germany** *(top);* **the 3/70 Armor, 5th Infantry Division, roll out of Coleman Barracks near Mannheim, Germany** *(middle);* **and Army equipment stored at Rhine Ordnance Depot** *(bottom).*

Above: The CH-47 medium-lift (bottom) and the XCH-62 heavy-lift helicopters.

Opposite: A recruit takes a break during basic training. Women, although excluded from combat, receive M16 rifle training.

artillery and tactics. Airplanes and antiaircraft guns were in use, as were gas and chemical projectiles. New tactics included barrage fire, destructive fire to destroy trenches and neutralization fire to prevent enemy action. The regular Army increased to a peak of four million, but quick expansion caused confusion and inefficiency. After the war, the army was restructured: troops were reduced to about 200,000, while the number of officers was increased and used to train the National Guard and reserves. For the first time, emphasis was placed on theoretical study.

Further technological developments brought changes in the nature of warfare during World War II. Increased firepower and mechanization reduced the need for soldiers on the battlefield. Only 30 percent of the air and ground strength was in combat units; support

personnel made up the remaining 70 percent. Women entered the Army as nurses and later as members of the Women's Army Corps (WAC), filling staff and technical jobs as noncombatants, releasing more than 350,000 men for combat-related assignments overseas. The Selective Service Act of 1940 helped the Army reach its peak strength of 11 million during the war, reduced to 571,000 after peace was restored. The draft was discontinued in 1949, but quickly reinstated in 1950 following the outbreak of the Korean War.

The US had severely reduced troop strength just prior to a plea for assistance from the United Nations. As part of the UN international force in Korea, the Army gained experience in antiguerilla warfare. The Army grew to 1,596,000 by 1952, but totaled less than 1 million by 1957.

In the 1950s and early 1960s, the threat of atomic and then nuclear war prompted the restructuring of combat divisions into more mobile and flexible combat forces for use in smaller scale conventional battle. The US entered

into the North Atlantic Treaty Organization (NATO) to ensure the postwar defense of Europe.

As a member of the Southeast Asia Treaty Organization (SEATO), the US agreed to help check the spread of communism in Southeastern Asia and became involved in the Vietnam conflict in the late 1950s. Army troop strength in Vietnam grew from a small group of special advisers to a peak of 365,000 in 1969. In December 1972, 23,000 remained, and in 1973 all ground troops were removed. During the war, the airmobile division was first put into service, using helicopters and airplanes to support ground combat units. The helicopter emerged as one of the most vital pieces of machinery used by the Army. It performed scout and attack missions as well as transported cargo and troops. Its speed and efficiency as an ambulance helped keep the mortality rate of American wounded at less than one percent.

In 1973, the draft was abolished and a major reorganization began. The WAC was eliminated in 1978 and women were integrated into the mainstream. The Training and Doctrine Command (TRADOC) was established with the mission to determine and implement the doctrine and organization of the Army. TRADOC began plans for a smaller, lighter, more mobile force for use in conventional warfare, which evolved into the Army's current modernization programs.

A PERSONNEL PROFILE

Two hundred years ago, a man could join the Army if he 'could bring his own musket and uniform, did not have sore legs, scurvy, scale head, ruptures or other infirmities, and was able to carry his own weapon.' Today the Army's requirements are a bit more stringent. In fact it is so selective that 50 percent of those who apply are not accepted.

With worldwide commitments and the lowest peacetime personnel level in 30 years, the Army needs only high-quality people who can keep a smaller Army strong. The Army's 8800 recruiters actively pursue intelligent, motivated men and women to fill these needs.

Today's soldier is better educated than ever before. The percent of recruits with high school educations has increased from 54 percent in 1980 to 90 percent in 1984, and entrance exam scores have increased steadily as well. The minimum goal for all officers is a bachelor's degree. The Army has an 'up or out' policy, implemented with yearly testing and evaluation, that weeds out the soldier who does not improve physically and mentally and continue to be promoted.

A breakdown of manpower data shows that of the 780,000 active duty personnel, more than 107,000 are officers and 671,000 are enlisted; 214,000 are black, 28,000 are Hispanic, and 28,000 are other ethnic minorities. Of the 80,000 women in Army uniform, 10,000 are officers. The Army Reserve constitutes another 96,000 officers and 440,000 enlisted, while the Army National Guard has 42,000 officers and 401,000 enlisted personnel. In addition, the Army employs 450,000 civilians in positions ranging from administrators to foundry workers and scientists.

As its people continue to improve, so does the Army; its people are the Army's most vital source of power.

Fresh-faced Army recruits during basic training. The quality of recruits has improved dramatically in the last decade, contributing to the overall strength of the current Army.

ORGANIZATION AND STRUCTURE

The United States Army is operated by the Department of the Army, one of the three military departments within the Department of Defense. The secretary of the Army is a civilian, appointed by the president and approved by the Senate. As head of the Department of the Army, he is accountable to the president through the secretary of Defense. The secretary of the Army conducts all affairs of the department, including its organization, administration and operation. The principal assistants to the secretary of the Army include the under secretary of the Army and various assistant secretaries, counsels and chiefs.

The Army Staff is the military staff of the secretary of the Army. Presided over by the chief of staff, it gives professional advice and assistance to the secretary of the Army and his assistants. It is responsible for the recruiting, supplying, equipping, organizing, training, mobilizing and demobilizing of the Army.

The chief of staff is the chief military adviser to the secretary of the Army and is responsible for the planning, development, execution, review and

Above: **Army troops disembark from an Air Force aircraft in Germany to participate in 'Reforger' readiness exercises.**

Opposite: **Light infantry divisions provide the Army with more flexible forces.**

analysis of the Army programs. He is the highest-ranking officer on active duty in the Army. He also presides over the Army general staff and the special staff.

The US Army consists of its headquarters — located in Washington, DC and containing the office of the secretary of the Army and the Army Staff — and the Army commands.

THE MAJOR ARMY COMMANDS

The US Army Forces Command (FORSCOM) is the largest of the Army's major commands. From its headquarters at Fort McPherson, Georgia, FORSCOM directs active Army and Army Reserve troops in every state but Hawaii, as well as in the Commonwealth of Puerto Rico and in the Virgin Islands of the United States. During a full mobilization, its total strength, including National Guard troops, would be more than 950,000, nearly two-thirds of the Army's total ground forces.

The commanding general of FORSCOM is responsible for the five continental US Armies (CONUSAs),

Above: **US Army Reserve soldiers on maneuvers. The Army is increasing its reliance on well-trained reserve troops.**

Below: **A member of the 9th Infantry Division during exercise 'Border Star 85.'**

the Third Army, all assigned FOR-SCOM active Army units and Army Reserve units. The commanders of the five continental Armies command the US Army Reserve and supervise the training of the National Guard within their area of supervision.

The five Continental Army areas are:
• First Army: headquarters Fort George G Meade, Maryland, responsible for the northeastern United States
• Second Army: headquarters Fort Gillem, Georgia, responsible for the southeastern United States, the Commonwealth of Puerto Rico and the Virgin Islands
• Fourth Army: headquarters Fort Sheridan, Illinois, responsible for the north-central United States
• Fifth Army: headquarters Fort Sam Houston, Texas, responsible for the south-central United States
• Sixth Army: headquarters Presidio of San Francisco, California, responsible for the western United States

Third Army, headquartered in Fort McPherson, Georgia, was reactivated in December 1982. It is unlike any other Army in Forces Command; its

mission is to quickly respond to situations threatening to US interests in Southwest Asia. Though part of FORSCOM, the headquarters Third Army is under the operational control of US Central Command (CENTCOM); if deployed, Third Army will be commanded by CENTCOM. Instead of a fixed structure of assigned units, Third Army selects specific forces to fill its current needs. Among those forces available to Third Army are the 82nd Airborne Division, the 101st Airborne Division, the 24th Infantry Division (Mechanized), the 6th Cavalry Brigade, Ranger and Special Forces units and many Reserve Component units.

The US Army, Europe (USAREUR), headquartered in Heidelberg, Germany, commands the Seventh Army (the Army's largest overseas combat unit), the US Army Southern European Task Force in Italy and Army forces in West Berlin. The United States, as a member of NATO, maintains the more than 200,000 Army personnel assigned to USAREUR in a constant state of readiness to deter armed aggression by Warsaw Pact forces. In the event of war, USAREUR would

transfer control of its combat forces to NATO's Central Army Group (CENTAG) while continuing to provide administrative and logistic support to its forces.

Eighth US Army is headquartered in Seoul, Korea. Along with other US armed services, it helps the Republic of Korea (ROK) to deter outside aggression in accordance with treaties between the US and the ROK. During wartime, Eighth Army would receive and ready forces for combat under the ROK-US Combined Forces Command.

US Army, Japan, headquartered in Zama, Japan, has about 2500 personnel who perform support and logistical operations for the Army in Japan and the western Pacific.

Western Command, (WESTCOM), headquarted at Fort Shafter, Hawaii, directs the 20,000 Army personnel in Hawaii. It is part of the US Pacific Command, which oversees American forces in Hawaii and the eastern Pacific.

Training and Doctrine Command (TRADOC) is responsible for the training of regular and reserve soldiers in preparation for war. TRADOC determines how the Army will fight, how it will be equipped and how it will be organized. Its headquarters are at Fort Monroe, Virginia.

Army Materiel Command (AMC) is headquartered in Alexandria, Virginia. It has the mammoth task of developing, providing and maintaining weapons, equipment and supplies to the Army and its commands. It has the largest budget of all Army commands.

Information Systems Command plans, installs, engineers, operates and maintains assigned Army communications, base communications and Army air traffic control facilities as well as the Army portion of the Defense Communication System. Its headquarters are at Fort Huachuca, Arizona.

Intelligence and Security Command, one of the smallest commands, has a worldwide structure. From its Arlington Hall Station, Virginia headquarters, it directs intelligence collecting, counterintelligence, production and security operations.

Health Services Command provides health services for the Army within the United States, and for other governmental agencies and activities as directed. Its headquarters are at Fort Sam Houston, Texas.

Above and below: **The Army maintains its flexibility with numerous training and readiness exercises, including simulated combat maneuvers** *(above),* **and large-scale joint-forces exercises such as 'Team Spirit,' held annually in Korea.**

28

Criminal Investigation Command, with headquarters in Washington, DC, conducts all Army major investigations, operates the Army's crime labs and provides personal security for Department of Defense and Department of the Army personnel.

Military Traffic Management Command (MTMC) directs the moving and storage of household goods of military personnel and manages military traffic, land transportation and common-user ocean terminal service within the continental United States. Its headquarters are in Washington, DC.

US Army Military District of Washington (USAMDW) provides base operation and support to the Army, Department of Defense and other government activities while defending assigned Department of Defense facilities.

US Army Corps of Engineers (USACE) directs the engineering, construction, operation and maintenance of Army and Air Force facilities worldwide. USACE develops, manages and executes the Army's Civil Works Programs, which involve engineering and real estate activities related to rivers, harbors and waterways. It protects and preserves navigable waters and assists in recovery from natural disasters.

THE ORGANIZATION OF COMBAT FORCES

The active Army force is made up of 17 combat divisions. Five are forward deployed, or most ready for combat; four of these are directed by US Army, Europe. and one is part of Eighth Army in South Korea. Eleven are stationed in the continental United States under Forces Command and one is based in Hawaii under the Western Command.

The division is the basic combined-arms unit. Under one command and

Below: **An on-line M1 Abrams prepares to attack simulated enemy positions during training exercises at Fort Bragg.**

Opposite: **A tank crew member during 'Border Star 85' exercises in Texas.**

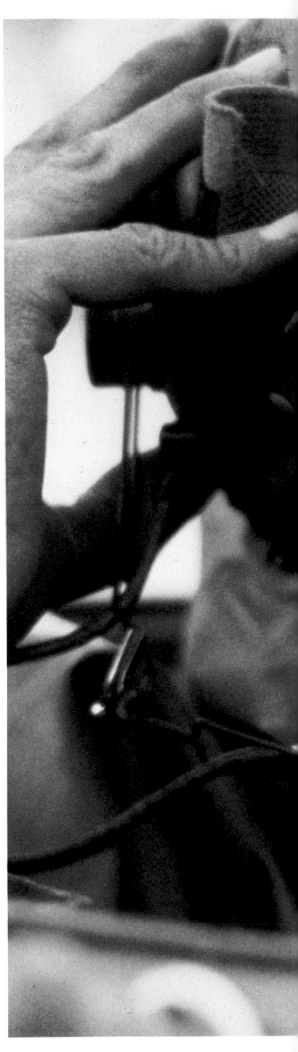

led by a major general, it is self-sufficient, containing support elements such as artillery, air defense artillery, intelligence, signal, chemical and engineer corps. Since it also includes combat service support elements such as transportation and medical services, it can function independently. However, for tactical reasons, two to five divisions often fight as part of a corps, which is commanded by a lieutenant general.

Each division contains six brigade-sized units, which are led by colonels. Each brigade is in turn made up of three to five battalions, the battalion being the basic maneuver unit, commanded by a lieutenent colonel and containing two or more companies of 150. Companies are led by captains and consist of two or more platoons of 40 men commanded by a lieutenant. Four squads (led by sergeants), the smallest combat units, make up a platoon. The number and types of battalions assigned by the command de-

Opposite: **One soldier seems pleased with his C-rations, the other not so sure.**

Below and overleaf: **Recruits in formation; and a soldier applies his buddy's camouflage make up.**

pend on force requirements determined by the the mission, the enemy and the terrain.

Light maneuver forces (light infantry, air assault infantry, airborne infantry and ranger infantry) are suited to close-in fighting in restricted terrain. Armor and mechanized forces maneuver well in open terrain, but are difficult to deploy and need considerable support once in the battlefield.

The Army does not have the airlift and sealift capability to deploy the most powerful and heavy equipment quickly in time of war, so it is restructuring light forces in order to meet its goal of greater strategic mobility. Light infantry divisions of 10,000 troops with fewer heavy weapons have been created that can deploy more quickly than the standard divisions of 16,000 men. A light infantry division can now be moved in 500 Air Force C-141 transports, compared to the more than 1000 it took to move a standard infantry division. Light divisions can be used as the primary force in low-intensity conflict, particularly in less developed areas of the world where no heavy forces are maintained. They can be followed by heavier forces if necessary and if the terrain warrants. They

would also be effective in mid- to high-intensity warfare as part of a corps force.

Armored and mechanized divisions are being redesigned for optimum use of new weapons and equipment, such as the Abrams M1 tank and the Bradley Fighting Vehicles, as well as for more rapid deployment. Troops are being cut from 19,000 to approximately 16,500. The modernization of heavy divisions is expected to continue into the 1990s as new weapons systems are fielded.

INFANTRY

The infantry, the largest combat arm, is the branch of the Army trained and equipped to fight on foot. Whether infantrymen march to battle, arrive by parachute, helicopter or ground vehicle, they attack and defend their position chiefly on foot.

There are two types of infantry divisions: light infantry, which is non-armored, and mechanized infantry, which travels in armored fighting vehicles.

Light divisions are a result of the Army's recent restructuring to deploy strategic forces more rapidly. They are

the smallest of all divisions, with an approximate strength of 10,000. A light infantry battalion contains about 380 men, structured in three infantry companies, one support company and a headquarters company.

Each solider carries his M16A2 rifle, which has replaced the automatic M16A1 as the Army's standard rifle. The M16A2 is lighter and can be fired in either a semiautomatic or three-burst automatic mode. In addition, easily portable weapons such as the MK19-3 grenade launcher, the M249 squad automatic weapon and the Dragon antitank missile are used by infantrymen. The Dragon is used in fewer numbers by light infantrymen as the emphasis now is on traveling 'light.'

Air assault infantry is a highly specialized force transported by helicopter, often past enemy ground defenses for the purpose of surprise attacks.

Airborne soldiers — paratroopers — are an elite group in the infantry. They are considered a strategic re-

This page: A US-Honduran air-drop exercise in Honduras. Honduran troops prepare to board C-130 transports *(top);* during the drop *(middle);* and a paratrooper awaits his jump *(bottom).* The Army conducts a variety of exercises in Honduras.

serve, since they deploy to critical areas quickly.

Mechanized infantry has high mobility and armor protection, and can fight — mounted or dismounted — as part of a combined arms force. Mechanized infantry divisions contain about 15,800 men. Each battalion has around 890 men, a headquarters and headquarters company, three tank companies and a support company. Some mechanized divisions are being restructured under the Division 86 system for easier deployment and have fewer troops.

The Bradley Infantry Fighting Vehicle (IFV) affords armored antitank protection to mounted infantrymen while keeping pace with mobile armor forces. Dismounted, infantrymen can provide close-in protection for tanks in restricted areas.

Infantry training is conducted at the US Army Infantry School at Fort Benning, Georgia, which has been 'home of the Infantry' since 1918. Future infantrymen are trained in the use of

This page: **US Army Rangers during training exercises. Ranger training is often conducted under physical and mental conditions more severe than actual combat in order to produce highly skilled and confident leaders.**

weapons and mines; armored carrier operations; individual and squad tactical maneuvers; patroling; first aid; map reading; communications; and nuclear, biological and chemical defense.

Airborne training is also conducted at Fort Benning. Paratroopers go through a demanding three-week course that prepares them for jumping into a battle zone, ready to fight.

Rangers are a unique class of infantrymen. They are specially trained to conduct decentralized, independent operations anywhere in the world and are transported to their destination via land, sea or air. Their presence is sometimes used to demonstrate US resolve. They can conduct reconnaissance missions and raids deep in enemy territory, arriving by parachute, small boat, Navy vessel or on foot. The US Army Ranger Department is located at Fort Benning. Selected volunteers are trained there and on four other bases that provide wooded,

This page: **Scenes from the National Training Center, where 'opposing forces' are outfitted and equipped as Soviets.**

Opposite: **Exercises often include simulated chemical defense training.**

mountain, desert and jungle/swamp environments. For 58 days and nights, they undergo demanding training under extreme mental and physical stress to prepare them for the cutting edge of battle.

The first Ranger unit, Roger's Rangers, was formed in New Hampshire in 1756 to fight with the British in the French and Indian War. Since then, units have been formed as needed by the Army. The number of Rangers assigned to Ranger units was increased in 1984 to 2300. In 1983, US Army Rangers performed bravely and effi-

ciently during Operation Urgent Fury in Grenada.

ARMOR

The armor branch is the Army's mounted combat arm and consists of the armor and armored cavalry units. The armored cavalry is the direct successor to the horse cavalry and performs many of its traditional duties, including security, ground reconnaissance and active combat. Cavalry units can force an enemy into terrain where the main armor units can attack. The

Above and opposite above: **Two Army helicopters: the AH-64 Apache, a powerful and agile antitank weapon; and the UH-60 Black Hawk utility helicopter, which has the principal mission of troop deployment and resupply.**

Officers and enlisted soldiers are trained for mounted combat at the Armor Center at Fort Knox, Kentucky. Hands-on training is emphasized and new techniques including laser firing are employed. Officers receive training in all crew duties before moving on to tactical exercises.

AVIATION

Bradley Cavalry Fighting Vehicle (CFV) is used for security and reconnaissance missions. It is replacing the M113A2 Armored Personnel Carrier as the primary vehicle for the armored cavalry. The size and configuration of cavalry units vary considerably. A cavalry squadron may or may not contain tanks and/or helicopters. Brigade-sized cavalry units are still referred to as 'regiments,' a throwback to the days when regiments of Army soldiers swept across the plains of the western frontier on horseback.

'Armor' means tanks. An armored battalion contains approximately 50 tanks, 550 officers and men, with a headquarters, headquarters company, three tank companies and a combat support company. Offensively, the M1 Abrams and the M60 tanks are used to penetrate the enemy's defenses or to outflank its forces. They are also used for rapid pursuit. Defensively, they maneuver rapidly to increase firepower where necessary.

Army aircraft play a vital part in modern warfare, as they fill combat, reconnaissance and transport roles. Attack helicopters, such as the AH-64 Apache, provide excellent strike and maneuver power, particularly when they work in conjunction with ground armor and cavalry units. Scout helicopters spot enemy positions and take aerial photographs. Small surveillance airplanes provide intelligence and communication to combat units. Utility helicopters, such

Right and opposite: Aircraft employed in combined arms combat training at the Army's National Training Center. The Air Force A-10 'Warthog' *(opposite)* provides close air support to ground troops, as does the AH-64 Apache attack helicopter.

as the UH-60A Black Hawk, are transportation vehicles. They move troops and equipment in and out of battle areas quickly. They are also used as ambulances. About 2000 personnel (10 percent women) are trained at Fort Rucker, Alabama in aviation-related occupational specialties, including mechanics, air traffic control and flight operations. To win his wings, an Army pilot must complete flight school at Fort Rucker, one of the most demanding training programs the Army offers.

FIELD ARTILLERY

The field artillery unit uses firepower to support the other combat arms, especially infantry, on the battlefield. It can neutralize enemy firepower and protect soldiers in a defensive position. Artillery units contain about 2300 troops and a

group of nuclear and nonnuclear weapons, including the howitzer canons, the Multiple Launch Rocket System (MLRS) and the Firefinder weapon-detection system. Artillery is transported by various means, from heavy trucks to utility helicopters such as the new UH-60A Black Hawk and the CH-47 Chinook. The Field Artillery Training Center at Fort Sill, Oklahoma annually trains 26,000 recruits in artillery-related occupational specialties.

AIR DEFENSE ARTILLERY

Air defense artillery units defend all ground forces against attack by enemy aircraft. To accomplish this mission, they employ several surface-to-air missile systems, including the shoulder-fired Stinger, the Chaparral, the Hawk and the Patriot.

Air defense training is conducted at Fort Bliss, Texas. About 8000 soldiers are trained there each year, a small percent of whom are women trained in support services.

COMBAT ENGINEERS

Engineer units play an important combat role. They provide essential construction to combat forces in the field. Often working under fire, they construct landing strips, bridges, roads and fortifications; they also emplace mine fields and obstacles. Engineering equipment, such as cranes, tractors and dump trucks, is often delivered to the unit by aircraft and is sometimes para-

Opposite page: **Army engineer training. National Guard combat engineers during road-building exercises in Panama** *(top);* **and** *(bottom)* **a welder at work. Welding is one of the many engineer occupational roles.**

Above: **The HUMMER (high-mobility, multi-purpose wheeled vehicle), a recently fielded one-and-a-quarter-ton truck.**

Below: **Combat engineers at work during training exercises in Panama.**

Above and below: Special Forces personnel in training exercises. Special Forces training is the most grueling of any in the Army and includes demolition work *(above),* as well as many arduous weeks spent in various terrains in preparation for their unconventional, independent style of warfare.

chuted in. In addition, units have floating bridges, inflatable assault boats and rafts.

Over 40,000 personnel are trained annually at Fort Leonard Wood, Missouri in various combat engineer occupational roles, such as engineers, plumbers, electricians, construction workers and vehicle operators and mechanics.

SPECIAL FORCES

The members of the Special Forces are better known as 'Green Berets' for their distinctive hats that set them apart from the Army at large. This elite group of rigorously trained men go where general purpose force cannot go. They conduct unconventional warfare in specially trained and organized units capable of independent operations. They are assigned to overt, covert or clandestine operations, in peace or war, that complement general purpose forces' capabilities. Their missions may involve strategic intelligence, psychological operations, Ranger operations, strike operations and related special operations. The First Special Service Force was formed in 1942, but the Special Forces lineage can be traced back to Rogers' Rangers, the first Ranger unit in America, which was formed 20 years prior to the Revolutionary War. The US Army Special Forces was established in 1952; many of its initial members were former Rangers who wanted further training in the unconventional type of warfare they had successfully used during World War II and the Korean War. They were looking for excitement, and they found it.

Special Forces training is the most extensive and the most demanding, physically and mentally, of any in the Army. After meeting stringent requirements including secret security clearance, soldiers spend from 24 to 58 weeks or longer training in swamp, jungle, amphibious, desert and arctic environments. Their preparation includes training in foreign languages and weapons, medical treatment and demolition.

Special Forces are also used in the area of foreign internal defense and nation building. As advisory groups, they help nations to build and train their armed forces.

Opposite: A member of the 1st Special Forces prepares to make a jump during 'Team Spirit' in Korea.

WEAPONS OF THE UNITED STATES ARMY

Today the Army is in the early stages of its weapons-modernization program. The present restructuring is expected to continue into the 1990s; the Army plans to field 400 new systems in the next 10 years. Following is a selection of some of the Army's key weapons systems currently in the field, categorized by the type of combat in which they are used.

CLOSE COMBAT WEAPONRY

Close combat involves the use of direct combat power at close range — weapon to weapon, man to man. The weapons employed in this type of fighting include tanks used by armored battalions; fighting vehicle systems and armored personnel carriers used by mechanized infantry; direct line-of-sight weapons and short-range mortars used by infantrymen.

The M1 Abrams tank is the Army's primary ground combat weapon system for closing with and destroying enemy forces by employing shock action, mobility and firepower. The M1 is used in conjunction with other ground and air systems under all battlefield conditions. The Abrams has special armor and a fire-detection and suppression system. Fuel and ammunition are stored away from the

Both pages: **The Night Chaparral, the type of Chaparral short-range, air defense system capable of night operations. In central Europe, Night Chaparral could operate 85% of the time.**

four-man crew. These factors make it less vulnerable and more survivable than its predecessors such as the M60 series. Its shoot-on-the-move capability and improved day-night fire control insure that it delivers accurate and lethal fire on both armored and unprotected targets. The 1500 hp turbine engine and improved suspension allow the 60-ton tank to move quickly across the battlefield at a top speed of 30 mph (top road speed, 45 mph), reducing the tank's exposure to enemy weapons.

The engine's high fuel consumption (a reported 1.9 mpg when first fielded in 1982) has been a target for the critics of the M1 program. However, the Army contends that the M1 is capable of operating through a 24-hour combat day without refueling. The tank has met the 275-mile-range requirements at 30 mph. The M1 uses about 32 percent more fuel, requiring more support vehicles, than the M60 series tanks, while its engine power is roughly 100 percent greater. The main gun of the M1 is the M68E1 105mm rifled gun, the standard main armament on US and most NATO tanks. The first production model of the improved M1, the M1E1, was produced in 1985 and features a 120mm smoothbore gun and NBC overpressure protective system. It weighs three tons

48

more than the M1 and is capable of a top road speed of 41.5 mph. In addition, the Army is pursuing a product improvement program to maintain the Abrams' competitive position through the 1980s and beyond.

The M60A3 is an improved version of the Army's M60 series tank, which has been in the field since 1961 and was the Army's main battle tank before the M1 was deployed. First-round hit capability has been enhanced for the

Previous page: **The M1 Abrams main battle tank** *(left)* **and the Bradley Fighting Vehicle. Mechanized divisions are being restructured to accommodate them.**

A3 by means of stabilization and the inclusion of a rangefinder, solid-state computer and thermal shroud. Fighting capability during periods of reduced visibility has been improved with the addition of the tank thermal imaging sight. M60A1 tanks are being converted to M60A3s throughout Europe and the US. The M60A3 weighs 57.3 tons and carries a crew of four at a maximum road speed of 30 mph. Its cruising range is 280

Both pages: The M113 personnel carrier, workhorse of the cavalry and infantry for many years, will be replaced by the Bradley Fighting Vehicle in most units.

miles at 20 mph, and it is equipped with the 105mm M68 rifled cannon.

The Bradley Infantry Fighting Vehicle (IFV) provides the mechanized infantry with a full-track, lightly armored fighting vehicle. It carries a nine-man squad, including a commander, gunner, driver and six infantrymen who can fight dismounted or mounted, using the six firing port 5.66mm weapons, the 25mm automatic stabilized cannon mounted in the two-man turret, the 7.62mm machine gun and Tube Launched Optically Tracked Wire Guided (TOW) antitank guided missiles.

The Bradley Cavalry Fighting Vehicle (CFV) is used by the scout and armored cavalry units for screening, reconnaissance and security missions. The structure is identical to the Bradley IFV, except for the absence of firing-port weapons. The CFV carries a five-man crew for reconnaissance missions. Both Bradley vehicles provide day and night thermal-sight capability for the commander and gunner, and image-intensification night-vision capability for the driver.

The M113 Armored Personnel Carrier was designed to transport troops, equipment and cargo during combat operations. The current M113A2 is being replaced by the Bradley in infantry-squad-carrier and cavalry/scout functions. The M113 will continue to be upgraded for use as a mortar carrier, command post, MED-EVAC carrier and maintenance support vehicle beyond the year 2000. The M113A2 is made of aluminum and weighs 12.5 tons. It carries 11 men at a road speed of 42 mph and cross-country speed of 19 mph. It has an 11 hp engine and features a 50-caliber machine gun.

The AH-64 Apache, the Army's primary attack helicopter, is a fast-reacting airborne antitank weapon. In wartime, it would be dispatched to the heaviest enemy penetration and destroy, disrupt or delay the attackers

Left: **The Vulcan antiaircraft gun, mounted on a tank chassis.**

Below: **An AH-1S modernized Cobra attack helicopter in current configuration.**

long enough for friendly ground units and armor to arrive. Its two-man crew can navigate and attack in the darkness thanks to a Target Acquisition Designation Sight and Pilot Night Vision Sensor (TADS/PNVS). It is also equipped with a 30mm chain gun and 2.75-inch rockets. The Apache's mission weight is 14,660 lb and it can travel at 146 knots. The Apache, deployed in 1985, is supported in the field by the Cobra.

The AH-1S Cobra (the newer version of the AH-1, which was used extensively in Vietnam) is an attack helicopter with the primary mission of destroying light armored vehicles. However, its performance is limited, and it is now used as a complement to the Apache. The Cobra TOW missile system requires that the target be kept in crosshairs until impact, leaving it vulnerable to enemy missile and gunfire. Also, the Cobra is mostly limited to fair-weather performance. The Army has begun the Cobra Fleet Life Extension (FLEX) program, providing

Below: **A UH-60 Black Hawk transport helicopter hovers over marshland. The UH-60 is a highly effective tactical assault vehicle. The Black Hawk is also used for aeromedical evacuation.**

improvements to keep the Cobra in service for some time to come. The Cobra weighs 10,000 lb, flies at a speed of 129 knots, carries a crew of two and features eight TOW missiles, 2.75-inch rockets and a 20mm cannon. Its endurance is 2.2 to 2.9 hours. The Cobra is the attack version of the Huey utility helicopter; both aircraft have been in service with the Army for 20 years.

The M249 Squad Automatic Weapon

is a lightweight, one-man portable base of fire for infantry squads. In the 1970s, this role was filled by the M16A1 rifle, which was equipped with a bipod and fired in the automatic mode. The M249 is more stable, accurate and has a higher rate of fire than the M16A1.

Below: **A variant of the M113 personnel carrier, modified to carry the Vulcan antiaircraft gun, being loaded with blue practice rounds.**

AIR DEFENSE WEAPONS

Air defense weapons are ground-fire systems used to detect and engage enemy aircraft. They protect all ground-force elements, including troop formations, depots, lines of communication, air bases, key command and control facilities.

The Chaparral, the Army's short-range defense (SHORAD) surface-to-air missile system, provides protection for forward-deployed divisions and corps and for rear-theater areas. A self-propelled, self-contained system, it has excellent cross-country mobility. The launch station is also self-contained and can be taken off the carrier and used from the ground. It is supersonic and lightweight, and has fire-and-forget capability as well as an infrared homing guidance system that can engage both approaching and receding targets. Its targets are visually acquired, which has posed a problem at night and in bad weather, but the addition of Forward-Looking Infrared (FLIR) night sight has improved visibility. Chaparral has an Identification Friend-or-Foe (IFF) subsystem, which helps the gunner identify friendly targets. It carries four ready missiles on launch rails and an additional eight missiles in storage.

The Army had high hopes for the Sgt York Division Air Defense (DIVAD) gun system as an eventual replacement for the Chaparral and the Vulcan in close-range, low-altitude air defense. However, it was canceled in production by Secretary of Defense Caspar Weinberger on 27 August 1985. Weinberger stated that the weapon's performance did not warrant the additional 3 billion dollars necessary to complete a project on which the Pentagon had already spent 1.8 billion dollars since 1978. The Sgt York (named after World War I hero Alvin C York) was designed as a mobile, radar-controlled, all-weather gun to provide air-defense coverage for maneuver troops against Soviet ground-attack aircraft and antitank guided-missile-launching helicopters. Extensive field testing in 1984 showed that the computerized aim of the Sgt York was not much better than the systems it was

Opposite above: **The Chaparral, a short-ranged air-defense missile system.**

Opposite below: **The ill-fated Sgt York air defense system, scrapped in 1985 for being over budget and under qualified.**

designed to replace and that it was quite vulnerable to attack by enemy aircraft. Each component of the system worked well separately — but not together — and the computer that coordinated the system tended to malfunction. Despite the critics' assertions that the weapon was too complex and expensive, the Army wanted to continue the project, believing that the technical problems could be worked out and that solving those current problems was preferable to waiting years for a new-generation antiaircraft gun to be delivered.

The Stinger, a shoulder-fired, heat-seeking, infrared homing-missile system, provides air defense to even the smallest units. It is designed to withstand the rigors of the battlefield and requires no maintenance in the field.

The Patriot is the Army's new, all-altitude missile system. It has fast-reac-

Above: **A soldier aims the Stinger, a 35 lb, shoulder-fired, man-portable guided-missile system that provides air defense against low-level aircraft.**

tion capability, high firepower and the ability to operate in a severe electronic-countermeasure environment. It requires less equipment, less operational manpower and fewer repair parts than the Hawk, the low- to-medium-altitude missile system that the Patriot was designed to replace.

FIRE SUPPORT SYSTEMS

Fire support systems generate indirect firepower. They include cannons, rockets, missiles, and target acquisition and communication systems.

The Multiple Launch Rocket System (MLRS) is a free-flight, area-fire, artillery rocket system with the

This page: The Multiple Launch Rocket System (MLRS), designed to complement cannon artillery in combat, can operate day and night in all types of weather. Its surface-to-surface free rockets have a range in excess of 30 kilometers, and a 12-rocket load can cover an area the size of up to six football fields.

Above and below: The Multiple Launch Rocket System (MLRS). The MLRS carries a crew of three that controls the system, whether the on-board fire control computer is on automatic or manual. The tracked mobile launcher has cross-country capability comparable to the M1 tank and can be part of a combined-arms, tank-led combat team.

primary mission of counterfire and suppression of enemy air defenses. It supplements cannon artillery fires by delivering large volumes of fire in short time spans. It was fielded in 1983.

The Army employs three howitzer cannons: the M109A2 and M110A2 self-propelled cannons and the M198 medium towed cannon. All are capable of launching a variety of nuclear and nonnuclear munitions.

The Battery Computer System (BCS) works in conjunction with the howitzers to provide improved fire control. The system consists of a computer terminal at the field artillery battery headquarters and a display unit at each weapon. The BCS receives firing-data requests, computes the data and sends it to each howitzer. The BCS can also be used with the MLRS.

COMBAT SUPPORT SYSTEMS

Combat support systems provide operational assistance to the combat arms. They include engineer support systems, which are used in combat engineer efforts and mine/countermine warfare, and theater tactical intelligence systems, which provide theater/tactical commanders with information to support planning, the readiness of forces for combat, and the conduct of combat operations.

COMBAT-SERVICE SUPPORT SYSTEMS

Combat-service support systems provide tactical units with maintenance, supply, medical, transportation and other vital services. They range from commercially available, four-wheel-drive trucks adapted for Army use to utility helicopters. Some primary weapons from this group are discussed below.

The Black Hawk UH-60A utility helicopter is used in air assault, air cavalry and aeromedical evacuation missions. It adds considerably to the Army's division mobility. In a single lift, it can reposition an 11-man fully equipped squad or a 105mm howitzer, its crew of six, and up to 30 rounds of ammunition. It is more easily maintained in the field than any other helicopter. It travels at 145 knots with

Opposite: **The crew of a UH-60 Black Hawk about to settle the big bird on a golden-brown field. The Black Hawk's missions include combat service support.**

an endurance of 2.3 hours and features two 7.62mm machine guns. The Black Hawk was first fielded in high-priority units in the continental US and Korea in 1984, and to WESTCOM and FORSCOM in 1985. During Operation Urgent Fury in Grenada, a Black Hawk reportedly took 45 rounds of groundfire and kept flying.

The CH-47 Chinook, the Army's medium-lift helicopter, is used to move ammunition, repair parts, petroleum, artillery, troops and special weapons. It has undergone major modernization programs since first being fielded in 1962. CH-47A, B and C models are being upgraded to the D model, which will expand the life of the fleet past the year 2000. The Chinook weighs 50,000 lb, travels at 158 knots and is capable of carrying 33 troops. Its maximum cargo load is 24,000 lb.

TACTICAL COMMAND, CONTROL AND COMMUNICATION SYSTEMS

The Tactical Command, Control and Communications C^3 systems allow a commander to locate and communicate with his tactical unit, even in an area with enemy electronic countermeasures. They range from a single channel ground and airborne radio system to the Defense Satellite Communications System (DSCS) for which the Army develops and fields satellite earth terminals for all the armed forces.

Above and below: **The CH-47 Chinook medium-lift helicopter carrying an external load, and a string of UH-60 Black Hawks on desert maneuvers.**

NEW TECHNOLOGIES

In order to be prepared for the 1990s and beyond, the Army is developing new 'leverage' technologies that may completely change the ways in which wars are fought. The Army's new thrusts in technology include dramatic improvements in battlefield information communications; self-contained munition technologies that will allow munitions to independently seek and home in on hostile targets; and biotechnology, which promises to improve the prevention and treatment of casualties and diseases through rapid identification, new vaccines and detection of chemical and biological agents. Enhanced hands-on training programs will improve operators' performance in the use of sophisticated equipment. These programs will underlie all new technology thrusts as well as ongoing engineering developments and product improvements.

The AH-64 Apache attack helicopter, silhouetted against a stunning sunset. Army helicopters are named after American Indian tribes.

TRAINING AND EDUCATION THE GOOD GET BETTER

The emphasis on state-of-the-art weapons does not overshadow the importance of the soldier; without a competent human to run it, the most sophisticated system is little more than a hunk of hardware. The benefits of a weapon are lost if the soldier doesn't completely understand it and the strategies involved in using it. A major challenge for the Army is to integrate new equipment with well-trained, intelligent, capable, combat-ready personnel.

The Training and Doctrine Command (TRADOC) has the complex and vital job of ensuring that soldiers are ready to fight and win whenever and wherever they are needed. TRADOC decides how the Army will fight as well as how it will be equipped and organized. TRADOC conducts training at 17 installations, 15 branch schools, 8 specialist schools, 3 integrating centers, over 1000 ROTC programs and the Command and General Staff College. Its 1984 training budget was 5 billion dollars. A variety of training programs is used to develop and maintain quality soldiers and officers. They range from Initial Entry Training to computer-simulated and live-com-

bat exercises. Initial Entry Training consists of Basic Training, Advanced Individual Training (AIT) and One Station Unit Training. Soldiers who will serve in noncombat arms receive Basic Training followed by Advanced Individual Training in their military occupational specialties, which may range from administration and finance to missile repair. Soldiers entering combat arms branches such as infantry, artillery, and armor receive One Station Unit Training, which combines basic and specialized training. Women are trained at five out of the eight Army training centers. Since by law they may not serve in combat arms or direct combat support, they continue on to AIT. Throughout his or her term of service, a soldier may be eligible for continued specialty training.

BASIC TRAINING

Basic Training transforms a civilian into a soldier in eight weeks. Soldiers are trained at platoon level, providing the opportunity for individual attention. The standard is excellence, not adequacy. Basic is divided into three phases. The first phase (two

Opposite: **Recruits stand at attention before their drill sergeant. The drill sergeant is responsible for the recruits' health and welfare during basic training.**

Left: **Prior to actual basic training, recruits spend a few days at a reception station, where the men receive a close shave and all are issued Army gear.**

weeks) covers basic soldier skills, from drill training to M16A2 rifle instruction and nuclear, biological and chemical warfare defense. The second phase (three weeks) includes weapons training and map reading; basic skills are reinforced and developed. In the last three weeks, tactical training, field training and the physical endurance confidence course are mastered. Emphasis is on teamwork and attitude. When the civilian has successfully become the soldier, he or she moves on to more advanced training in a particular Army occupation.

OFFICER TRAINING

Several paths can be followed by the man or woman who wishes to be an Army officer:
- Reserve Officers Training Corps (ROTC)
- The United States Military Academy at West Point
- Officer Candidate School
- Direct commission (civilian with special skill)

ROTC is the largest source of officers for the Army, providing about 70 percent of the Army's officers annually. ROTC students join the program while attending college. After graduating and being accepted for duty, he or she enters Officer Basic Course (OBC), which prepares lieutenants for duty in active and reserve units. They are taught to lead, train and fight, and are qualified for branch duties. The 20-week Officer Advanced Course (OAC) prepares the officer for unit command in his or her future branch. Combat leaders learn to move, shoot and communicate; combat support leaders learn to lead support troops. For example, OAC students at the armor school in Fort Knox concentrate on tank-company command, tactics and combined arms doctrine. The signal school teaches electronics, computers and tactical communications devices. All OACs include hands-on tactical training in preparation for leading soldiers in combat.

Since it was founded in 1802, the United States Military Academy at

From top: **The path of potential soldiers. A young man at the crossroads; Army recruits are sworn in; and, any recruit's final destination, Basic Training. The recruit at left is discovering that the discipline begins before he's even off the bus. He has eight more rigorous weeks ahead.**

Above: A drill sergeant offers a word of advice to a recruit at Fort Campbell, Kentucky. Many soldiers remember their 'DI' with respect, if not fondness. Anyway, they remember him.

Below: Recruits on the march. From basic training to computer-simulated battle and overseas force deployment exercises, the Army provides tough, realistic training.

Below: Mud-caked but jubilant infantrymen of the 2nd Infantry Training Brigade, Fort Benning, Georgia after completion of a confidence course. These soldiers are undergoing One Station Unit Training, in which the unit stays together through basic and advanced training. The recruit giving the 'thumbs up' sign *(left)* can be seen battling the course in the inset *(opposite below)*.

An aerial view of the United States Military Academy at West Point, looking north up the Hudson River. West Point is the site of the oldest continuously occupied military post in the country. Its strategic location in a narrow 'S' turn on the Hudson made it ideal for General George Washington's headquarters in 1779.

Above: **The US Military Academy's Battle Monument at Trophy Point.**

Opposite: **The Cadet Chapel of West Point after a picturesque snowfall.**

West Point has produced a long line of distinguished alumni including Ulysses S Grant, Douglas MacArthur, Dwight D Eisenhower and astronaut Edwin 'Buzz' Aldrin. Today, West Point graduates about 900 officers a year, providing excellent academic training as well as military training. Preparation for a military career includes field and classroom instruction in military skills, an intensive physical education program and practical and classroom training in leadership. During the academic year, military instruction is limited to two hours per week of theory and classroom work; however, the summer months are devoted to practical, in-the-field military training. After completing the four-year program, the cadet enters service with the Army as a second lieutenant and is trained by the branch to which he or she is assigned.

The Army's Officer Candidate School trains enlisted men who are college

Above and overleaf: **Cadets march in front of Washington Hall; hats fill the air as West Point cadets celebrate their graduation with the traditional signal.**

graduates or obtaining a degree. They receive 22 weeks of training before advancing to OCS and OAC.

Certain professionals may be offered a direct commission as an Army officer. Doctors, nurses, lawyers and chaplains are in demand and may receive commissions based on their training.

Other training opportunities are available to officers after they have spent time as commanders or staff officers. The Combined Arms and Services Staff School offers an intensive course that emphasizes staff skills for a variety of missions in combat, combat support and combat-service support units. The Command and General Staff College prepares field grade officers for the responsibilities of command and staff.

Portraits of women in the Army: A drill sergeant advises a recruit during basic (*left*); a recruit combats an obstacle course (*top*); a Military Police officer communicates by walkie-talkie (*middle*); a paratrooper after completing her jump (*bottom*). Women are an integral part of the Army, filling ranks from private to general. Career opportunities are available to women in all occupational specialties not directly combat related. A small percentage of women, who will be involved in support services, are eligible for airborne training.

Above: **US Army Rangers prepare to be airlifted to a remote area for maneuvers.**

Left: **A wooden tower is used to simulate rappelling out of helicopters.**

COMBAT TRAINING

The lack of realistic combat training prior to actual combat has cost many lives throughout the Army's history. Today, various types of combat training exercises — from simulations to the full deployment of units overseas — are used to test and improve combat readiness.

The Army participates in many large-scale exercises throughout the world: 'Reforger' is an operational maneuver and training exercise that takes place in Germany. US-based active and reserve forces deploy to Europe, where they train in what could be their wartime environment. Similarly, Third Army deploys to Egypt for 'Bright Star' exercises every other year.

The National Training Center (NTC) at Fort Irwin, California is unique among training centers. Its size and scope allow for the training of task-force battalions whose weaponry has grown beyond the limits of other centers in the nation. NTC offers a vast

Above: **A smiling 'wounded' soldier is evacuated during training exercises.**

Right: **A drill sergeant instructs a recruit on the M16 rifle range.**

maneuver space, well-trained opposing forces (OPFOR), live fire, an instrumented battlefield and standardized, computerized evaluation. Perhaps the NTC's most unique feature is the OPFOR, who are dressed in Soviet uniforms and whose weapons are modified to look like Soviet weapons.

Since space and live munitions are not always available to meet the expanding training requirements, battle simulators are seen as an economical yet highly effective alternative to 'live' training. The Army training battle-simulation system (ARTBASS) is an automated, interactive system for maneuver battalion commanders and their staffs. By 1987, the aviation combined-arms team training (ACATT) computer simulator will provide total, combined training to the scout, attack team and battle captain while saving fuel, ammunition and hours. The use of computerized battle simulators is increasing as systems become more sophisticated, and they will be heavily relied upon in the future.

A soldier is schooled in the use of aerial photos during a field training exercise. Maneuvers are intended to be as close as possible to the real thing.

Above: Mechanized infantrymen run alongside a Bradley Fighting Vehicle during an exercise at the Infantry Training Center at Fort Benning.

Below: Combat training involves high tech, such as the position location reporting system *(left)*, and old-fashioned crawling under barbed wire *(right)*.

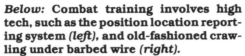

Below: Rangers man a mortar position during field maneuvers. The number of Rangers has increased recently as the Army restructures itself to meet the ever-changing threats it faces.

Opposite: Trainees engaged in hand-to-hand combat. The soldier of today is better trained than ever before in basic combat skills, as well as in the evolving concepts of modern warfare.

Above and opposite: Portraits of 'Border Star 85.' A member of the 9th Infantry Division, which demonstrated a frontal assault at the Donna-Anna range north of El Paso, Texas *(above)*; and Pvt Darren Rollinson, M60 tank crew member.

Above: Comprehensive training in nuclear, biological and chemical warfare defense is vital to every soldier's safety.

Below: A soldier in a tight spot during Ranger training.

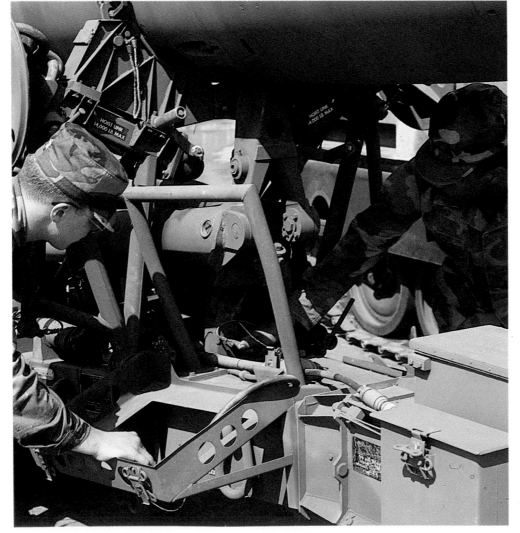

Numerous types of training programs are available to Army personnel. Soldiers and officers alike may spend time cracking a book *(above)*; or receiving hands-on technical training, such as that offered at the Redstone Arsenal in Alabama *(left)*. Academic and technical training not only further military careers, but promise broader civilian employment opportunities.

EDUCATION

The Army sets high standards for its people; then it helps them to achieve these standards. Today's soldier should not only be combat-ready, but knowledgeable and highly motivated. The Army Continuing Education System (ACES) helps soldiers and officers to improve their skills, and therefore their success in and out of the Army, with many levels of programs — from basic reading to doctoral degrees.

Unfortunately, some soldiers do not possess the basic reading, writing and mathematical skills necessary to advance in the Army. Basic skills are taught to these soldiers, and those who do not have a high school diploma are strongly urged to acquire one by taking the high school equivalency test or enrolling in classes offered on their bases.

Top and above: **SFC Curtis explains the intricacies of the land combat support system to Pvt Blowe at Redstone Arsenal, Alabama; a soldier fine tunes television equipment in an Army TV studio.**

Above and above right: **A soldier at work at her computer terminal; and learning the fine points of operating a radar scope. Much of the Army's technical training is transferable to civilian careers. The Army's**

training and education programs promise that the good get better, and women can and do fill critical positions in all components except active combat which is not allowed by law.

Throughout their careers, all soldiers and officers are encouraged to further their education. Officers are now required to have a bachelor's degree, and an officer is not usually able to achieve the rank of major without a master's degree. The Army pays a percentage of tuition (up to 90 percent) at civilian schools, depending on rank and length of service. High school, college and graduate courses can be taken through the mail by personnel unable to attend classes for reasons of logistics or scheduling.

Each Army base has an education center that assists personnel in achieving their education goals. Material and facilities are provided so that soldiers can work alone or in a group to increase their knowledge in their Military Occupational Specialty (MOS). Military correspondence courses are available as well. Education centers help in preparation for the Skill Qualification Test (SQT) taken annually by most enlisted personnel. SQT results figure heavily in promotion and re-enlistment considerations. In fact, a low score on the SQT, followed by no improvement, can result in a discharge from the Army. In 1984, 25 percent of Army personnel allowed to re-enlist

would not have met the re-enlistment standards without assistance from the education and training programs.

The Army teaches vocational-technical skills, such as computer programming or auto mechanics, for on-the-job or personal use. An apprenticeship program documents work in specific jobs for use in obtaining civilian employment if and when a soldier leaves the Army.

With the educational opportunities afforded today's soldiers and officers, it is not suprising that in a recent survey the major reason for joining the Army was 'to get a good education.'

THE UNITED STATES ARMY IN ACTION

Two recent military involvements illustrate both the effectiveness of the Army's light forces and the need for improved capability to engage in low-level conflict.

Light, flexible and highly mobile troops were used with great success during Operation Urgent Fury in Grenada; conditions in Central America show the advantage of structuring troops to handle low-intensity conflict effectively. To this end, special forces and Ranger units are being expanded and more light infantry troops organized to deal with this continuing threat.

GRENADA

On 25 October 1983, President Ronald Reagan ordered US Army and Marine forces to the tiny Caribbean island of Grenada to rescue nearly 1000 Americans thought to be in danger in the wake of a bloody Communist coup. Marxist Prime Minister Maurice Bishop had been murdered by members of the 'Revolutionary Military Council' led by General Hudson

Opposite: **A member of the 101st Airborne ('Screaming Eagles') studies a map during 'Bright Star' exercises in Egypt.**

Right: **Infantrymen use camouflage gear and natural foliage for cover in combat.**

Austin, and the nation was in chaos. The US military operation, called Urgent Fury, had an urgent mission: prevent a repeat of the 1980 Iran hostage situation.

Grenada had been a British possession until 1974, and in 1979 Bishop overthrew the newly formed government and established relations with Cuba. US intelligence reports of Soviet and Cuban military projects, including military training areas, storage facilities for ammunition and supplies as well as a runway capable of accommodating Soviet long-range offensive aircraft were released in March 1983. In October, the military council, which controlled Grenada's 2000-man army, had closed schools and nonessential businesses and set a four-day, twenty-four-hour 'shoot on sight' curfew.

Near dawn on 25 October, US Army Rangers from the 1st and 2nd battalions of the 75th Infantry parachuted onto the Point Salines Cuban-built airfield, located on the southern tip of the island and surrounded by water on three sides, at some points as close as 35 feet. With no reserve parachutes, the Rangers jumped in at 500 feet to better avoid hostile gunfire. Amid unexpectedly heavy antiaircraft fire, the first two US Air Force C-130 transports were forced to abort their approaches.

86

Above and left: **The 82nd Airborne played a large part in the Grenada rescue/invasion in 1983. After securing Salines Airport on Grenada, they moved out on patrol** *(above).*

The third aircraft sneaked in during a short lull and dumped about 50 Rangers onto the 10,000-foot runway. They alone fought Cuban and Granadian forces for 20 minutes, as a resurgence of antiaircraft fire kept the last four C-130s from closing in. The stranded Rangers quickly radioed nearby AC-130 Spectre gunships, which suppressed enemy fire long enough to allow the rest of the Rangers to jump.

After landing, the Rangers — still

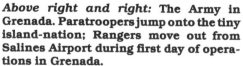

Above right and right: The Army in Grenada. Paratroopers jump onto the tiny island-nation; Rangers move out from Salines Airport during first day of operations in Grenada.

under fire — cleared the runway of barbed-wire barricades, rollers, trucks and bulldozers, while the 1st battalion secured the northeast end of the airstrip where the enemy had established positions in building foundations and houses. Within approximately two hours, the Rangers had secured the airport, enabling US Air Force C-141s carrying two battalions of the 82nd Airborne Division to land. Meanwhile, Marines of the I-84 Amphibious Group had secured Pearls

Airport, a commercial airstrip at the northern end of the island.

At dawn the next day, 82nd Airborne troops attacked a compound of 10 to 15 concrete buildings in the hills one mile north of the airstrip. They were met with heavy sniper fire, which they returned with M-203 HE rounds. Failing to locate the source of enemy fire, they called in Navy A-7 Corsairs to strafe the compound area. The defenders surrendered, but not before several US soldiers were wounded.

Heavy casualties were prevented at one point in the rescue/invasion by a quick-thinking soldier. His unit was trapped in a house surrounded by Cuban forces; using his AT&T long-distance credit card, he telephoned Army officers in Fort Bragg, North Carolina and informed them of the

Opposite: **82d Airborne troops prepare to move out from the Salines Airport.**

Below: **UH-60 Black Hawks damaged during Operation Urgent Fury on Grenada. Three were disabled on 27 October.**

unit's dangerous position. Fort Bragg contacted the Air Force, which sent in AC-130 Spectre gunships to disperse the Cubans and relieve the unit.

Also on 26 October, Army and Marine forces combined in a heliborne assault on the Grand Anse campus of St George's Medical College, rescuing over 200 students. One student provided the world with on-the-spot action reports via his ham radio for more than 30 hours, relaying accounts of students rolling under beds and diving into bathtubs to avoid stray bullets. The following day, more than 200 additional students were rescued on the Lance aux Epines peninsula. Although some students later insisted that they were in no danger, most expressed gratitude to the US forces for their courageous undertaking.

Hostilities officially ceased on 2 November, but more than 2000 US troops still remained to clear out snipers and hidden Communist-made weapons. By December a few hundred US troops remained in Grenada in an

advisory capacity. In all, 18 US troops were killed and 116 were wounded.

HONDURAS

The presence of US troops in Honduras has been a subject of heated debate since the first group of Green Berets arrived in March of 1982 to train Honduran soldiers guarding their border with El Salvador. In 1980, the US had begun military aid to the government of El Salvador in the form of 35 million dollars and 20 Green Berets as military advisers in El Salvador's struggle against revolutionary guerilla troops. The US felt it had the evidence to support its claim that the troubled country was in danger of becoming a Soviet satellite.

Fearing involvement in another Vietnam-type conflict, many members of Congress and US citizens have objected strongly to US military presence in Central America. Nevertheless, it continues, and the Army plays a large

role in that presence in Honduras. In 1985, about 1200 Army personnel were on temporary duty in Honduras as part of Joint Task Force Bravo, the headquarters and support element for the joint US-Honduran training exercises that take place regularly in that country. Joint Task Force Bravo is headquartered at the Honduran air base at Palmerola; there are six or seven additional bases and small airstrips in Honduras that are also used by US troops.

Ongoing training exercises range greatly in size, emphasis and dura-

tion. The 'Big Pine' exercises have involved as many as two thousand US soldiers at one time. A recent road-building exercise, 'Cabana 85,' lasted three months and involved mostly engineer troops. 'Big Pine III' brought US tanks to Honduras for the first time. Some counterinsurgency training lasts only a few days and involves fewer than 100 troops. Army forces, aside from the support troops, include special forces and active and reserve combat units that are deployed to Honduras to train and be trained.

The Defense Department gives three

reasons for the US presence in Honduras. To demonstrate US resolve in Central America and to improve Honduras' capacity for self-defense, while providing a place for US troops to train for low-level conflict. The Army will be in Honduras in this capacity as long as the US-Honduran agreement benefits both countries.

Previous page: **MPs listen for intruders during maneuvers.**

Above: **A paratroop drop during training exercises in Honduras, and a soldier gives the thumbs up sign to a driver.**

Below: An Army truck is guided aboard an Air Force C-5 Galaxy in Honduras. The Army plays an integral part of the controversial presence of US troops in Honduras.

Below: Honduran troops board a US Air Force C-130 transport plane for deployment to their training site. US-Honduran training maneuvers are commonplace in Honduras.

Above: Camouflaged infantrymen aim
their M16s. Infantry training includes
individual and squad tactical maneuvers
as well as patrolling.

Overleaf: Army Reserve infantrymen undergo exacting nuclear, biological and chemical warfare defense training, while on tactical maneuvers.

Below: The Corps of Cadets assembled on the Plain at the US Military Academy.

THE
US NAVY
TODAY

THE US NAVY TODAY

THOMAS YORK

62

Previous page: The USS *New Jersey* (BB62) in San Francisco Bay during the celebration of the 40th anniversary of the end of World War II.

Below: The USS *Hercules* (PHM 2) hydrofoil, heavily armed with eight Harpoon missiles and a 76mm gun, has a speed of over 40 knots when foilborne and a range of over 1200 nautical miles if hullborne. This ship and its *Pegasus*-class sisters have faced controversy because, for all their speed and maneuverability, they are extremely expensive to build for their size and range.

INTRODUCTION TO THE UNITED STATES NAVY

'Our status as a free society and world power is not based on brute strength. When we have taken up arms, it has been for the defense of freedom for ourselves and for other peaceful nations who needed our help. But now, faced with the development of weapons with immense destructive power, we have no choice but to maintain ready defense forces that are second to none. Yes, the cost is high — but the cost of neglect would be infinitely higher.'

(President Ronald Reagan at the recommissioning of the USS *New Jersey* on 28 December 1982 at the Long Beach, California, Naval Shipyard.)

The United States Navy today is the largest and most powerful armed force on the high seas. Established more than 200 years ago to protect the maritime interests of the 13 American colonies, it remains a critical component of the nation's defense strategy. Its advanced fleet power of 37 nuclear-powered ballistic missile submarines (SSBN), unique undersea vessels developed and pioneered by the Navy, is the maritime leg of the the US nuclear defense triad that includes

The Navy looks to tomorrow. Seamen aboard the USS *New Jersey* (BB 62) *(opposite)* and the sailor with a sextant *(above)* can look forward to manning warships fitted with the most modern of weapons.

long-range bombers and intercontinental ballistic missiles (ICBM). The US Navy also boasts the fourth largest air force in the world, with more than 6000 fighters, support aircraft and helicopters in its inventory. The only challenger on the high seas is the Soviet blue-water navy, a growing menace to US naval supremacy around the globe.

It is a navy in transition. Neglected during the Vietnam era of the 1960s and allowed to decline in the 1970s, the Navy is experiencing renewed attention in the 1980s. Billions of dollars are being spent to build dozens of new ships for the fleet. At the beginning of the decade, there were just over 450 ships in the Navy, compared to a World War II high of about 2500. The present number is about 550. The goal is to deploy 600 ships at the end of the decade.

The Navy today is a flexible and sophisticated armed force designed to protect and defend the United States at sea. The major portion of the surface fleet is divided into battle groups structured around the Navy's 13 deployable aircraft carriers. These include four of the largest warships in the world — one *Enterprise*-class and

The flags are out for a port call to San Francisco aboard the USS *New Jersey* (BB 62). Its 16-inch guns saw action in WW II and Vietnam, but the ship was 'mothballed' until its recommissioning in 1982. This *Iowa*-class battleship can serve as an integrated part of a Carrier Battle Group, spearhead assault force or lead its own Surface Action Group.

three *Nimitz*-class carriers. These carriers are supported and protected by a fleet of battleships, cruisers, destroyers, frigates and submarines. Many of them are nuclear powered.

The battleships are an unusual feature of the modern Navy. Once believed to be obsolete, the World War II-era *Iowa*-class batleships have been reactivated and rearmed with advanced armament and antimissile defense systems. Three battleships, the USS *New Jersey* (BB 62), the USS *Iowa* (BB 61) and the USS *Missouri* (BB 63) have already been recommissioned. A fourth, the USS *Wisconsin* (BB 64), is scheduled to be brought out of mothballs and recommissioned by the end of the decade. The very high accuracy of their 16-inch guns and the lethal effect of the massive projectiles make the *Iowas* four of the most effective conventional fighting ships in the world today.

The other warships of the fleet are fitted with the latest in defense technology and weaponry on the high seas. Vessels with advanced electronic countermeasure and missile defense systems include the *Ticonderoga*-class cruisers. They are armed with the computerized Aegis air-defense system, which can direct and control up to 18 ship-to-air missiles against high-density air attacks from Soviet antiship cruise missiles.

Sophisticated *Spruance*- and *Kidd*-class destroyers and the sleek *Oliver Hazard Perry*-class frigates also contribute to making the US Navy the most advanced in the world. Dozens of other warships and support ships play prominent roles. Among them are amphibious-warfare ships and helicopter-landingcraft carriers, as well as numerous support vessels from mobile logistic ships to under way replenishment ships.

In addition to the ships of the fleet, nearly 2500 fighters and attack aircraft and their weapons systems are on duty and ready for action. These include the A-6E Intruder all-weather carrier-based attack planes and the new F/A-18 Hornet multirole tactical aircraft. The Navy's versatile F-14 Tomcat fighters are armed with Phoenix missiles effective at ranges up to 100 miles. Other weapons systems include the Harpoon air or surface-to-surface missiles, Tomahawk tactical antiship and land-attack missiles, acoustic-honing antisubmarine-warfare (ASW) torpedoes and attack and ASW shipborne helicopters.

Officers welcome Vice President George Bush aboard the USS *Enterprise* (CVN 65) on a beautiful August 1985 day. On any day, however, their distinguished visitor would find the ship in top maintenance. The weapons department seaman *(opposite)* spruces up an anchor with practical rust preventive paint.

ORGANIZATION AND STRUCTURE OF THE UNITED STATES NAVY

The US Navy was established on 13 October 1775 when the Continental Congress enacted legislation that created the Continental Navy of the American Revolution. Later, following ratification of the Constitution, the Department of the Navy and the office of the secretary of the Navy were established by an act of Congress on 30 April 1798.

The Department of the Navy is one of three military departments—Army, Navy and Air Force—in the Department of Defense. Each is headed by executive department secretaries, who do not have cabinet rank. The secretary of the Navy, who is responsible for the Navy's overall readiness, has his office, like those of the other secretaries, at the Pentagon, in Arlington, Virginia, just a few miles from the White House. The secretary has several aides, including a civilian undersecretary, a deputy undersecretary and various assistants. The chief of naval operations is an admiral and the secretary's principal naval advisor. He commands personnel within the Navy and Marine Corps as directed by the secretary.

The Department of the Navy is divided into three major components: the Navy Department, the Operating Forces and the Shore Establishment. The Navy Department comprises the central offices and bureaus of the executive arm of the Department of the Navy which are located in Washington, DC.

The Operating Forces include sea commands such as the Atlantic Fleet, headquartered at Norfolk Naval Base, Virginia; the Pacific Fleet, headquartered at Pearl Harbor Naval Base, Hawaii; and US Naval Forces, Europe, headquartered in London, England. The Pacific Fleet consists of the Third and Seventh Fleets. The Second Fleet is assigned to the Atlantic Fleet and the Sixth Fleet is assigned to the US Naval Forces, Europe. Each of these smaller, numbered fleets defends a separate geographic area.

The Second Fleet operates in the western Atlantic Ocean, with Norfolk, Virginia the home port of the flagship.

The Sixth Fleet operates in the Mediterranean Sea, with Gaeta, Italy the home port of the flagship.

The Third Fleet operates in the middle and eastern Pacific Ocean, with Pearl Harbor, Hawaii the home port of the flagship.

The Seventh Fleet operates in the western Pacific Ocean, with Yokosuka, Japan the home port of the flagship.

The numbered fleets are divided into task forces. Organization of these forces is flexible, depending upon the requirements of the Navy. The commanders in chief of the major fleets direct the several subordinate commanders who control various types of groups and forces. Generally, each subordinate commander has control of a single type of ship, such as submarines, and is handed responsibility for developing tactics and doctrine as well as providing manpower, spare parts and safety standards to the fleet. The naval reserve force is responsible for the organization, training and mobilization of reserve ships, aircraft and personnel.

Two additional major naval operating forces are the Military Sealift Command (MSC) and the Naval Reserve Force. The MSC is operated by the Navy for all services and consists of ships manned by civilian government employees and commercial ships employed on a contract basis. The ships are used to transport service personnel and their dependents, combat troops, supplies and materiel to all parts of the globe.

The Shore Establishment provides support to the fleets and other operating forces by training personnel as well as supplying and maintaining material and equipment. It includes naval districts, naval bases, ammunition depots, hospitals, training commands, communications and intelligence.

The Shore Establishment consists of various commands, including the Bureau of Naval Personnel, Naval Medical Command, Naval Oceanography Command, Naval Space Command, Naval Legal Service Command, Naval Telecommunications Command, Naval Intelligence Command, Naval Investigative Service, Naval Education and Training Command and Civilian Personnel Command.

The Bureau of Naval Personnel plans and directs the procurement, distribution, administration, and career development of Navy active duty and reserve personnel, while the Naval Medical Command directs the provision of medical and dental services for the Navy and Marine Corps.

The Naval Oceanography Command is a functional field command coordinated by the commander of Naval Oceanography and the superintendent of the US Naval Observatory. Its programs cover the science, technology, engineering and operations essential to exploring the ocean and the atmosphere and to providing astronomical information and time estimates for naval operations. The Naval Oceanographic Program, for instance, is responsible for the physical sciences of hydrography. It collects data for the charting of the oceans and establishes geodetic references for navigation. This program also studies underwater acoustics, water dynamics and corrosion, as well as meteorology and astronomy. These studies are used to calculate precise geodetic positions on the globe and to establish the precise time of day required for navigation.

The Naval Space Command oper-

The Midshipman Drum & Bugle Corps in spiffy dress and polished brass perform during the commissioning of the nuclear-powered strategic missile submarine USS *Ohio* (SSBN 726) on 11 November 1981.

Although the decks may not always be made of teak (as they are on this battleship), swabbing them will always be part of the regimen of daily life for Navy seamen.

ates space systems, such as satellites, to support US forces worldwide, while the Naval Legal Service Command administers legal services programs. Naval Telecommunications is responsible for telecommunications systems, while Naval Intelligence is responsible for security and intelligence gathering. The Naval Investigative Service commands law enforcement, criminal investigative and counterintelligence support. Naval Information Systems is responsible for the administration and coordination of computer data information systems, while the Civilian Personnel Command oversees the management of the 350,000 civilian employees of the Navy. Naval Education and Training provides shore-based education and training.

TRAINING AND EDUCATION OF NAVY PERSONNEL

The Navy's mission is to remain ready to conduct operations at sea in support of US political and military interests close to home waters and abroad. This responsibility is carried on the shoulders of its 565,000 men and women, in conjunction with the support of the US Marines. The sophisticated ships, submarines and aircraft of the Navy call for highly skilled and trained individuals. In fact, in recent years more than 90 percent of the Navy's new recruits have earned high school diplomas before joining the service. To prepare the thousands

of men and women for their tasks, the Navy has established dozens of schools and training programs ranging from basic training to PhD programs affiliated with major colleges and universities.

The premier educational facility for the Navy is the US Naval Academy at Annapolis, Maryland. Founded in 1845 as the Naval School, the academy today admits 1200 men and women each year, most of them from high schools across the nation. The academy offers 18 majors in the subjects of engineering, science and math. Upon graduation, each midshipman receives a bachelor of science degree and then undertakes at least five years of service in return for the privilege of getting a college education. Each candidate must obtain a nomination from any of several possible sources, including nominations from US congressional representatives in the district where the applying candidate lives. The candidate must also qualify scholastically, medically and physically.

The Navy also administers a Naval Reserve Officers Training Corps program in more than 63 colleges and universities throughout the nation. About 1400 officers are commissioned annually in these programs. In addition, the Navy operates postgraduate schools for masters and doctoral pro-

A Navy color guard and drill team trains long hours for its performance (below), and the recruits (opposite) listen to long hours of indoctrination lectures about the Navy.

grams, with 800 graduates receiving degrees each year. It participates in graduate programs in more than 50 schools across the nation, including such prestigious schools and universities as Harvard University, The Massachusetts Institute of Technology, The University of California and Stanford University. Some 400 degrees are conferred in these programs, in subject areas ranging from religion to nuclear physics. A professional war college, staff college, and medical school are also operated by the Navy.

It is possible for enlisted personnel to advance to the officer's rank by successfully completing the proper educational programs in the service. Below the officer ranks, the Navy offers a two-year, associate-degree-granting program for about 2500 enlisted men and women annually through participating colleges and universities. An enlisted commissioning program annually gives degrees to about 200 sailors who have two years of college education in the sciences or arts.

In addition to basic training for all enlisted personnel, the Navy offers several advanced training schools. There are dozens of these schools located at bases and training facilities throughout the Navy.

There are 565,000 men and women in the US Navy. All are volunteers since the US military no longer uses the draft to supply its manpower needs.

While the great majority of the Navy's personnel consists of men, many stationed on warships, an in-

creasing number of women are taking up important roles at shore facilities and on selected ships in the modern Navy. Women are forbidden by federal mandate from serving on warships, but they are allowed to serve on support ships such as submarine tenders, oilers and supply ships. There are more than 41,000 women in the enlisted ranks, or 8.5 percent of the total number of people in the enlisted ranks, while there are more than 6600 women serving in the officers' ranks, or 9.6 percent of the total number. Although they are restricted from combat roles, there are no barriers to education or advancement in the Navy. Women can be found at all levels, from basic recruits to admirals. Women serve in such roles as public relations officers, administrators and instructors.

Twelve percent of the Navy's sailors and officers are black Americans, while more than 3 percent are Hispanic Americans. Other minorities

This page: **Recruits aboard the training destroyer USS *Recruit* (TDE 1) get instructions and then try them out. Here they** **practice mooring, but they will also learn anchoring, block and tackle, and other basic seamanship skills.**

account for nearly 6 percent of the total for both officers and sailors.

SHIPBOARD ORGANIZATION

US Navy ships are supplied with enough officers and enlisted personnel of various grades and ranks to operate and fight efficiently. Ships are organized for war, with the idea that crew assignments can be changed or expanded quickly when conditions warrant. Such organization is based on a grouping of functions and personnel intended to minimize duplication or overlap of command responsibilities.

Any officer in command of a ship, regardless of rank, is called the captain, but he is known as the commanding officer (CO). Based on centuries of tradition, his authority is absolute, within bounds of the Navy regulations. The CO is totally responsible for the operation, safety and appearance of

the ship he commands, as well as the health, morale, and welfare of his crew. Other responsibilities include the safe navigation of the ship, condition and appearance of materiel and personnel, proper stationing of trained lookouts and preparation of the ship for battle. The CO may delegate these responsibilities, but delegation does not relieve him of the responsibility for the ship.

During combat, the CO is required to engage the enemy and fight to the best of the ship's ability, and he must not disengage the ship until the fighting is completed. The commanding officer's battle station is that station where the action can be best fought. In case of the loss of the ship, both custom and regulations require that the CO assure that abandon-ship procedures are completed. All personnel should be off the ship before the CO abandons ship himself.

The executive officer (XO) is the next in the chain of command aboard ship. If the CO is absent, disabled,

Above: **Recruits receive training on various exterior parts of an aircraft. The over 565,000 personnel in the Navy started at this point at one time.**

relieved from duty, or detached without relief, the XO assumes command. He is also responsible for helping to maintain the general efficiency of the ship. With the assistance of the heads of the departments, he arranges and coordinates all of the work, drills, exercises, personnel organization, and the policing and inspection of the ship.

Assisting the XO are several assistants, such as the personnel officer, the training officer, the educational services officer, the substance abuse coordinator, and the command master chief.

Each ship in the Navy follows a standardized organization divided into departments, with the number of departments included in a shipboard organization dependent on the type and size of the ship. Departments are grouped together as either command

or support departments. In most cases, an officer heading a command department is a line officer eligible to exercise command in the event of the loss of superior officers. In aircraft carriers, the operations and air departments are headed by naval aviators.

Warships with ordnance, such as gun batteries, torpedoes, missiles, etc, have a weapons department headed by a weapons officer. Some surface warships with combat systems and some classes of submarines have combat-systems departments headed by combat systems officers. Ships not dependent on ordnance have deck departments usually commanded by first lieutenants. Aircraft carriers and some other ships have a weapons or combat-systems department in addition to a deck department. Under the weapons or combat-systems officers, the department is responsible for the operation, care and maintenance of the ship's armament and weapon-fire-control systems.

Above: **Enlisted men aboard a tank-landing ship on bridge watch.**

Right: **LCDR Lukinbeal serving as officer on deck on the bridge of his vessel.**

The weapons department operates the guns, torpedoes, fire-control systems and sonar. This department also keeps the ship's side and other exterior surfaces painted and clean. The deck hands of the weapons department are experienced in block and tackle, anchoring and mooring, running the ship's boats and other chores of seamanship. Gunner's mates and fire-control technicians are responsible for arming and firing the guns and tracking and killing submarines.

The operations department handles such communication functions as electronic warfare and intelligence gathering from the radar and radio systems. The information is collected, displayed and passed along to those who are responsible for guiding and fighting the ship. Its electronics tech-

nicians operate and maintain the electronic equipment. Radarmen operate the air- and surface-search radars. Quartermasters and signalmen are responsible for visual communication on the bridge.

The engineering department runs the engine plants that provide power to the ship and furnish electricity for the guns, radar, radios, air conditioning, and other auxiliary machinery. The engineering officer may be assigned several assistants, such as the main-propulsion assistant, damage-control assistant, and the electrical officer.

The supply department is responsible for feeding and clothing aboard ship. The galley, mess hall and general storerooms are operated by cooks, bakers, commissarymen and storekeepers. Disbursing clerks maintain pay records. The supply officer operates the laundry, ship's store, fountain, and barber shop.

The medical department is responsible for maintaining the health of personnel of the command, and routinely inspects the ship's food service, as well as living, berthing, and working spaces to make sure they are sanitary. The dental department is responsible for the dental care and oral health of the ship's personnel.

Navy aircraft-squadron organization differs from shipboard organization, with each squadron divided into an administrative department and a safety department. Most also have operational and maintenance departments. The administrative department handles all administrative chores within the squadron, such as official correspondence, personnel records and directives, while the safety department is responsible for all matters concerning the squadron safety program. The operational department is responsible for the operational readiness and efficiency of the squadron. The maintenance department maintains the aircraft. Combined, the squadrons assigned to each ship form a wing.

The division is the basic unit of the shipboard organization, and ship divisions are divided into watches or sections. The number of divisions in a department varies among ships, and the number of personnel in a division may be only a few or as many as 200.

Required aboard each ship are such documents as a standard organization and regulations manual, a battle organization manual, and a watch

Above: **Crewmen sweep down the helicopter deck of the battleship USS *Iowa* (BB 61).**

Opposite: **Taking weather readings is but one of the many operations within the Naval Oceanography Command.**

and station bill to ensure a well-coordinated team. These documents outline in detail for each ship the assignment of officers and enlisted personnel.

Ships are operated according to conditions of readiness or alerts, ranging between Condition Watch I, the maximum state of readiness when crews have been sent to battle stations prepared for fighting, and Condition Watch V, when the ship is in port. Each ship has a battle bill—the organized plan for action against the enemy. It lists the stations that must be manned under battle conditions and shows personnel requirements for manning those stations. These assignments are made according to billet numbers, rather than individuals. Division officers take into account personal qualifications, then assign crew members to billets and enter their names on the divisions' watch, quarter and station bills.

Aboard ship, security watches are stood to prevent sabotage, to protect property from damage or theft, to prevent access to restricted areas and to protect personnel. Included in the watches are sentry duty, barracks watches, fire watches and watches stood under way. The watch system is divided into two parts, when the ship is in port and when it is under way. Key assignments include the command duty officer, the officer of the deck, jun-

ior officer of the deck, junior officer of the watch and combat information center watch officer.

A ship's deck log is a daily record, by watches, of activity aboard the ship—events and occurrences that concern the crew and the safety of the ship. The ship's navigator is responsible for keeping the log. Accuracy is very important, because such entries often constitute important legal evidence in judicial and administrative fact-finding proceedings for incidents involving the ship and its crew. Information in the log includes such facts as the ship's operating orders, its courses and speeds, positions, state of the sea and weather, damage to the ship or its cargo, deaths or injuries to personnel, records of meeting or courts-martial and other formal boards, as well as changes in ship personnel or passengers. An engineering log is also kept pertaining to the important events and data of the propulsion plant.

The space provided for the officers' living quarters usually is located near the wardroom. This is the part of the ship known as 'officers' country.' If there is room, senior officers are assigned individual staterooms. Junior officers and warrant officers usually share staterooms or are assigned to a bunkroom, while petty officers are bunked in large compartments containing tiered bunks and metal lockers.

Eating aboard ship is divided by rank. On flagships there are usually six messes. The flag mess is held for the admiral, while the captain's mess is for the captain. The mess in the wardroom is held for the other officers, except warrant officers who eat with the chief petty officers. The general enlisted mess is held for all enlisted personnel except for chief petty officers. Enlisted men are given their food by the government; officers must pay for their food since they are paid a subsistence allowance to cover the cost of meals. On small ships, messes are combined.

Ships of the US Navy are usually divided into three classes: combatants, auxiliaries and service crafts. The bulk of combatants are warships, ranging from the mighty nuclear-powered aircraft carriers to fleet-patrol ships. Auxiliary ships include oilers, ammunitions ships and store ships, as well as tenders, transports, cargo ships, repair ships and salvage ships. Service ships range from harbor tugs to floating derricks and dry docks.

THE FLEET OF THE UNITED STATES NAVY

DEPLOYMENT

The United States has become increasingly dependent upon trade with its friends and allies since the end of the Second World War. Ninety percent of all international trade is carried by ship. With so much of this international trade carried across vital sea lanes, maritime strategy has become critical to the United States. Protection of the sea lanes is a major reason Navy warships are deployed so far from home ports. The Navy has the responsibility of deterring attacks on the US from the sea and ensuring unimpeded use of ocean trade routes in times of hostility. This responsibility has spurred the Navy to maintain equality with the Soviet navy—its principal potential opponent. The Soviets have deployed increasing numbers of warships and submarines throughout the major oceans of the world.

In the Pacific, Soviet ships could threaten at any time to cut off the flow of material and supplies from America's trading partners in the Far East such as Japan, Taiwan and Hong Kong. They also could threaten to sever the flow of oil carried by ship from the

Opposite: **The awesome striking power of 16-inch guns aboard this Navy battleship protects the carrier in the background, the USS** *Enterprise* **(CVN 65).**

Above: **An F-14 Tomcat from the 'Jolly Rogers' squadron aboard the carrier USS** *Nimitz* **(CVN 68) makes a low-altitude turn above two nuclear-powered guided missile cruisers under way. The F-14 protects the fleet from air attack.**

Alaskan oil fields to the continental United States.

In the Atlantic Ocean, the Soviet navy poses an ever-present threat to the United States and its allies of the North Atlantic Treaty Organization (NATO). During 1984, in the waters of the Barents, Norwegian and North Seas, the Soviet navy held the largest exercises ever conducted in Europe. More that 200 ships participated, not including more than 70 submarines, which pose a vital threat to shipping and surface ships in the event of hostilities. The Soviet Union now has more than 270 attack submarines in her fleet. In 1942, during World War II, Germany almost shut down the Allied flow of materials and supplies across the Atlantic with fewer than 60 submarines. The US Navy currently has about 200 active surface-combatant ships and 100 active submarines in its fleet.

To guard US interests on the high seas, the Navy maintains a high degree of readiness for action in regions where combat could be expected in time of war, such as the Mediterranean Sea and the Indian Ocean. Typically, two carrier groups are stationed in the Mediterranean and two in the

Below: An aerial port quarter view of the battleship USS *New Jersey* (BB 62)—at upper left—under way with ships assigned to her Central American task group: a fleet oiler *(top center)*, a cruiser *(far left)*, and frigates including the USS *Knox* (FF 1052) *(lower left)*.

Below right: The USS *Mars* (AFS 1) combat store ship carries two CH-46 Sea Knight helicopters and is armed with four 3-inch/50 caliber guns. Most of the seven *Mars*-class ships are less than 20 years old and in excellent condition to respond to additional requirements placed on the Navy's auxiliary forces.

western Pacific. They are backed by carrier groups and other support ships based at ports in the United States. Other surface groups are deployed at strategic stations throughout the world.

Navy surface ships are usually organized around carriers, amphibious or replenishment ships, with the number of defending battleships, cruisers, destroyers, and frigates greatly exceeding the number of ships being protected. For instance, 20 to 30 combatant ships are often grouped together to provide cover to unarmed landing ships as they are moved to landing areas under hostile conditions. The same number can be expected to escort replenishment ships to forward areas to keep fighting ships on station in times of hostilities. Other ships would be needed to protect convoys carrying troops, supplies and materials. Some of these defense responsibilities are handled by attack submarines, which would be responsible for antisubmarine warfare (ASW) duties during hostilities. Up to three submarines are assigned to each task group constructed around a carrier.

Others are assigned the duties of protecting the larger and more vulnerable Poseidon and Trident submarines as they patrol waters far from their home bases.

CARRIERS

The first carrier specifically designed to carry and launch aircraft joined the US Navy in 1934. However, the importance of the carrier to modern naval warfare was not established until World War II when the Japanese ably proved the capability of the carrier-launched air attack at Pearl Harbor on 7 December 1941. Aircraft from the carriers sank or severely damaged a number of major US warships lying at anchor in the harbor. In the naval actions that followed in the Pacific Ocean, US carriers became the critical instruments of war in establishing military superiority over the Japanese. But as carriers developed in size and capability in the postwar era, they became controversial and their futures were challenged. In spite of the fact that carriers have been called upon dozens of times to successfully carry out military actions since the end of World War II, opposition to them has been loud. Opponents argue that they are too costly to construct and lack adequate defenses. They say thay are vulnerable to both nuclear and conventional weapon attacks. Despite this debate, the carriers of the US Navy remain the principal military force on

The flight deck crew (above) of the nuclear-powered carrier USS Carl Vinson (CVN 70); and four F-14 Tomcats (right) over the carrier USS John F. Kennedy (CV 67), which is conventionally powered.

Work aboard carriers includes maintenance on an A-7 Corsair II *(above)* on the USS *Midway* (CV 41) and monitoring gauges in the machine room *(below)* on the USS *America* (CV 66).

Right: An 'easy' catapult launch of an F-14 flying 'hands off.'

Opposite below: The USS *Nimitz* carries some of its 90 aircraft on deck.

the high seas and will remain so well into the next century. All US carriers constructed since 1964 have been nuclear powered.

The backbone of the Navy fleet are the nuclear-powered carriers, with the six carriers of the *Nimitz*-class among the largest warships in the world today. Four are currently deployable: they are the USS *Nimitz* (CVN 68), the USS *Dwight D Eisenhower* (CVN 69), the USS *Carl Vinson* (CVN 70) and the USS *Theodore Roosevelt* (CVN 71). Each has an overall length of 1092 feet and deck width of 252 feet and they

each displace over 93,000 tons when fully loaded with aircraft. Each ship can steam up to 33 knots with power supplied by two large nuclear reactors and four sets of turbines. They carry more than 90 aircraft and helicopter, many of them equipped to deliver nuclear attack weapons. In spite of the awesome fire power of the squadrons aboard the carriers, defenses are minimal. Along with the other US carriers, the *Nimitz*-class carriers are lightly armed, fitted with three Phalanx close-in weapons systems, Sea Sparrow missiles and 20mm antiaircraft guns

Carrier flight deck operations can include arming a 250-lb bomb *(above)*; launching aircraft from the deck *(below)*; and stand- **ing ready during vertical replenishment operations by a CH-46 Sea Knight helicopter *(opposite)*.**

as their only defense. They rely on their fighter aircraft and attack bombers for long-range protection.

Two more carriers in this class are under construction or planned: the USS *Abraham Lincoln*, expected to join the fleet in 1989, and the USS *George Washington*, expected to join the fleet in 1991 and replace the USS *Coral Sea*. These are expected to be the last carriers, large or small, to be funded and constructed for some years to come by the United States. Many Congressmen are reluctant to fund more of them because they believe the massive ships can be easily immobilized and sunk. The complement of men on the *Nimitz*-class carriers is 3300, with another 3000 in the air wing on board.

The one ship of the nuclear-powered *Enterprise* class, the USS *Enterprise* (CVN 65), is slightly smaller than the *Nimitz*-class carriers. Displacing 89,600 tons fully loaded, she was constructed with eight nuclear power plants, rather than four, for propul-

135

After World War II carriers became the
most important ships in the fleet. The
Indian Ocean Task Force *(below)* from
back to front: the USS *Nimitz* (CVN 68).
USS *Midway* (CV 41) and USS *Kitty
Hawk* (CV 63); the USS *Ranger* (CV 61)
(bottom right); the maintenance crew
working on an F-4 Phantom on deck *(top
right)*; and the superstructure of the USS
Coral Sea (CV 43) *(overleaf)*.

sion. The first large nuclear-powered
surface warship constructed, she was
commissioned in late 1961. Like the
Nimitz-class designs, she carries more
than 80 aircraft and helicopters. She
carries a complement of 3100 men and
2400 in the air wing.

The single carrier USS *John F
Kennedy* (CV 67) of the *John F
Kennedy* class was originally intended to be nuclear powered. However, she
was laid down with a conventional
power plant because of a debate in
Congress over the cost of nuclear warships in the 1960s. She displaces
82,000 tons fully loaded, and carries
approximately 85 aircraft. There are
3100 men in the ship's company and
2400 in the air wing.

The USS *John F Kennedy* closely
resembles the carriers of the *Kitty
Hawk* class: the USS *Kitty Hawk* (CV
63), the USS *Constellation* (CV 64)
and the USS *America* (CV 66). They, in
turn, closely resemble the ships of the
older *Forrestal* class: the USS *Forrestal* (CV 59), the USS *Saratoga* (CV
60) and the USS *Ranger* (CV 61). All of
these ships were constructed in the
1950s and 1960s. The *Kitty Hawk*-
class ships displace 80,800 tons fully
loaded and carry 85 aircraft, while the
Forrestal-class carriers displace 75,900

to 79,300 tons and carry approximately 70 aircraft. Both classes have a
ship's company of 2800 men and 2150
in the air wing. All are armed with Sea
Sparrow missiles and the Phalanx
close-in weapons system.

The *Forrestals* were the first carriers to be constructed after World War II
in the years between 1952 and 1959
and they were the first to have angled
decks—a British invention. The USS
Forrestal was the first carrier designed
to handle jet aircraft from its decks.

All of the older carriers in the fleet
have been updated and improved or in
some cases completely overhauled.
Designs of the newer generation of
carriers have taken advantage of the
lessons learned in operating the older
carriers. For example, operational
weaknesses of the *Forrestals* were cor-
rected in the *Kitty Hawks*, most nota-

bly the location the deck lifts. These were constructed at the forward end of the angled deck in the *Forrestal* class. This position interferes with the launching and landing of the aircraft. Beginning with the USS *Kitty Hawk*, all US carriers have been constucted with a port deck lift moved aft to a point where it no longer encroaches on the angled deck. The carriers can launch and recover many aircraft without the lifts hindering deck operations.

The World War II-era *Midway*-class carriers, the USS *Midway* (CV 41) and the USS *Coral Sea* (CV 43), are the smallest and oldest carriers in the fleet, displacing just 64,000 tons with a full contingent of 75 aircraft on board. Other ships constructed in this class have been retired or used for aviation training. They were the first modern warships that could not pass through the Panama Canal because of their wide size. Originally constructed with straight decks of pre-war design, they have since been modernized so that they now have angled decks and advanced radar and large deck-edge lifts. The complement of men on the

Carrier personnel can truly see the world. The USS *Enterprise* (CVN 65) sails near a tiny fishing boat in the Philippines *(opposite)*; and the USS *Nimitz* (CVN 68) views the beckoning lights of Monte Carlo *(above)*. Yet the sailor *(below)* would probably agree there's 'no place like home.'

USS *Midway* and USS *Coral Sea* is about 2700, with 1800 in the air wing.

The Navy expects to have 15 carriers in its fleet by 1991. To extend the life of its older carriers without building costly new ships, the Navy has launched a program to overhaul major systems in eight of the oldest carriers. The Service Life Extension Program (SLEP) will extend the service life of the carriers from 30 to 45 years.

AIRCRAFT

Aircraft carried aboard carriers, or 'loadings,' vary according to size and mission. Loadings often include two fighter squadrons of F-4s or F-14s or a squadron of F/A-18s and one of A-6s. They also include one anti-submarine-warfare squadron of H-3 Sea King helicopters, RA-5C reconnaissance and EA-6B electronic warfare aircraft, KA-6 tankers, and E-2 airborne early-warning and control aircraft.

The F/A-18 Hornet, the first completely new tactical aircraft in the Navy in more than a dozen years, is three times as reliable as other fighters and features twice the warfare capability. It is also 20 times safer to fly than the aircraft of 30 years ago. It will ultimately replace the F-4 and the A-7 in both the Navy and Marine squadrons.

F-14 Tomcats, the Navy's fastest combat planes, rest on deck awaiting new missions *(opposite)*; two A-7Es from light attack squadron 82 in flight above the USS *Nimitz* (CVN 68) *(above)*; and the nose of an A-6E Intruder peeks from behind a tow tractor working on the USS *John F Kennedy* (CV 67) *(below)*.

It can carry up to 19,000 lb of armament, track multiple targets on its radar and attack eight targets with its air-to-air missiles. Instrumentation in the cockpit has been replaced with essential information displayed at eye level so the pilot can keep his attention on the targets. More than 1300 are planned for the fleet and the Marines.

The F-14 Tomcat is the Navy's most versatile aircraft. These fighters proved themselves in August 1981 when they were attacked by two Libyan aircraft over the Sidra Gulf. The two Tomcats evaded the attackers and downed both with a minimum of effort. The F-14's advanced radar system enables it to track 24 targets at once and attack 6 with Phoenix missiles while scanning the airspace for more targets, which can be destroyed up to 100 miles away.

The F-4 Phantom II is an all-weather defense fighter that flew for the first time in 1958. It has become the backbone of many foreign air forces, including those of Great Britain, Germany, South Korea, Spain, Greece, and Turkey. Production was stopped in 1979 after more than 5000 had been built for the Navy and Air Force. After two decades of service in the fleet, the A-7 Crusader is being replaced with the F/A-18. The A-7 was first flown in 1965.

The A-6E Intruder has been the medium-attack, all-weather mainstay of the Navy and Marine Corps for more than 20 years. It is used for close-in air support and deep-strike missions. Only the aging B-52s of the US Air Force can carry more payload. The A-6E can carry more than 30 types of bombs, rockets, missiles and mines, as well as Harpoon missiles and laser-guided weapons. It is updated constantly with advanced electronics packages.

The EA-6B Prowler is designed for tactical electronic warfare. It is primarily used to jam enemy defense systems during aerial combat. The E-2C Hawkeye is an early-warning aircraft equipped with advanced radar capable of detecting targets within 300 miles and tracking more than 250 aircraft at the same time.

The H-3 Sea King is equipped with sonar, active and passive sonar buoys, magnetic anomaly-detection equipment, and electronic-surveillance-measures equipment to give added protection against missile attack. This helicopter is being phased out in the last half of the 1980s. It has been flown for more than 20 years.

The F-14 *(opposite)* is the Navy's best fighter-interceptor while the F/A-18 *(above)* is its best fighter-bomber. A launch officer *(below)* signals one of them for takeoff from the flight deck of the USS *America* (CV 66).

A 'Wolfpack' crewman from VF-1 squadron hustles by one of the F-14 Tomcats
aboard the USS *Enterprise* (CVN 65).

Left: The starboard side of the USS *New Jersey* (BB 62) reveals the bridge, forward stack, 5-inch gun turrets and the Vulcan Phalanx close-in weapons system (the white domed object at top center).

Below right: Seamen aboard the same vessel lounge by the aft number three 16-inch turret.

BATTLESHIPS

Reactivation of the *Iowa*-class battleships has permitted the Navy to rapidly expand its fleet without costly new construction. The huge USS *New Jersey* (BB 62) was reactivated into service at less than half the cost of constructing a new frigate. Operating with a carrier battle group and surface-action group, the *New Jersey* is capable of destroying hostile surface targets and shore targets. In amphibious groups, the *New Jersey* can provide protection to other ships in the group, prelanding shore bombardment and additional gunfire support. Although constructed in World War II, the *New Jersey* and her sister ship the USS *Iowa* (BB 61) are not considered old or worn out since both saw limited service and were then 'mothballed' to preserve them. In fact, they are younger than the average ship in the fleet. The USS *New Jersey* has just 13.7 years of service, while the USS *Iowa* has seen only 12.6 years. The historic USS *Missouri* (BB 63), which is scheduled to rejoin the fleet in 1987, has seen just 10.1 years. The USS *Wisconsin* (BB 64), which will return to the fleet in the late 1980s, has just 11.3 years of service.

The four ships in the class are behemoths, displacing 58,000 tons at full load and carrying a crew of about 1900 men. They are almost 888-feet long and 108-feet wide, and are capable of cruising at 33 knots. They have a very long steaming range of 15,000

nautical miles at 17 knots. The most prominent feature of the *Iowa*-class battleships are the three sets of 16-inch main battery guns—two foward and one aft—the largest caliber guns in the world today. (Two Japanese battleships sunk during World War II had 18.1-inch guns.) Each of the nine guns, with well-trained crews, can hurl a 2700-lb piercing projectile on target 20 to 21 miles away every 30 seconds. The projectiles will penetrate 30 feet of reinforced concrete.

The *Iowa*-class battleships are the most heavily armored US warships ever constructed, designed to survive surface-to-surface engagements with enemy ships. The main armor belt consists of 12.1-inch thick steel at its thickest point. Turret faces are 17-inches thick, with tops 7.25-inches thick. Second deck armor is 6-inches thick, while the three-level conning tower sides are 17.3-inches thick.

Interestingly, until the battleships were reactivated, no production facilities were available to manufacture and assemble the 16-inch ammunition

Left: **Crew at work below a 16-inch gun turret on an *Iowa*-class battleship.**

Below: **The armor on the pilot house, 17.3-inches thick, can stop any artillery round or a tactical nuclear weapon.**

used by the guns. In addition to new ammunition now in production, there remain thousands of projectiles and charges in storage manufactured during World War II and the Korean War. This stockpile included 12,500 rounds of full-service charges, 12,600 rounds of reduced charges, 15,500 rounds of high-capacity projectiles (which contain less steel and more explosives than the armor-piercing rounds), and 3200 rounds of armor-piercing projectiles. Rounds fired in Vietnam were manufactured in the 1930s and were still in outstanding condition.

The USS *New Jersey* fired 771 main battery rounds during World

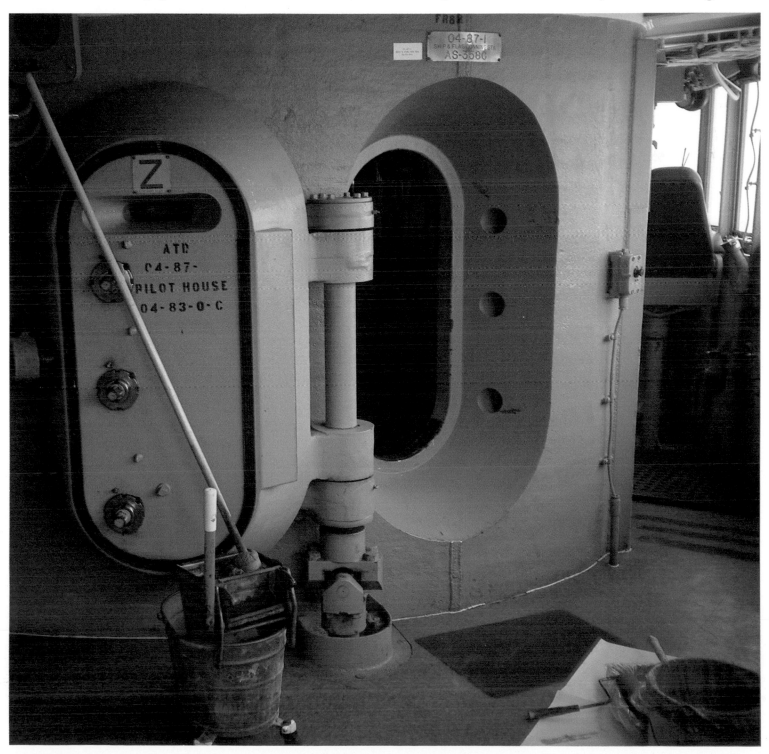

The dawn of a new day backlights the forward main turrets of this battleship beautifully photographed by ship's photographer PH2 Rick Sforza.

War II, 6671 during the Korean War and midshipman courses, and 5688 rounds during the Vietnam conflict. Some 15,000 rounds of 5-inch/38 ammunition were fired from the ship's 10 secondary batteries during its deployment to Vietnam in 1969. An inventory of more than 700,000 rounds of 5-inch/38 ammunition was still available in 1982. The semiautomatic, dual-purpose guns fire at a normal rate of 15-rounds per minute, but the gun's capability for rapid fire can be increased to 22 rounds per minute with a good crew.

The actual range of the 16-inch guns depends on the condition of the large barrels. The USS *New Jersey's* nine barrels averaged 42 percent wear when the ship was reactivated in 1982. The barrels were to have been replaced during the Vietnam War, but wear was greatly reduced with the use of a 'Swedish additive'—a material similar to a Teflon garbage bag was wrapped around the charges to reduce friction in the barrel. In addition to the barrels already installed on the four battleships, 33 barrels remain in storage.

Above: These seamen well know that painting a ship is a never-ending chore.

Right: The USS *New Jersey's* bridge is its nerve center. During WW II it was the flag bridge when the *New Jersey* was Adm Halsey's flagship, but battleships can no longer be designated flagships.

Each turret is manned by 77 personnel with up to another 36 personnel in each of the turret's six magazines. The large numbers are needed because almost all projectile and powder handling is largely done by hand and machinery.

Despite their awesome firepower, the battleships have been refitted with modern defensive protection, which includes new gunfire-control computers and target-designation systems. Eight Tomahawk armored-box launchers holding 32 cruise missiles have been added to give long-range protection. They have a range of 250 nautical miles when armed with conventional warheads and a modified Harpoon guidance system. The land-attack version with conventional warhead has a 700-mile range and with nuclear warhead a 1500-mile range. The missile

uses an inertial-navigation system with terrain-contour matching for guidance. In addition to the battleships, the Navy's cruisers and *Spruance*-class destroyers are getting the same modern defensive system.

For medium-range protection, the battleships are armed with four-canister Harpoon launchers carrying 16 surface-to-surface missiles for ship killing. The range of the missile is 70 nautical miles with high-explosive warhead. It searches for the target with its own radar while cruising at about 100 feet above the water. At the end of its flight, it executes a 'pop-up' maneuver to evade close-in enemy defense systems. This also enhances the effectiveness of its warhead. The *Iowas* have also been fitted with four Vulcan Phalanx close-in weapon systems for close-in antimissile defense. This impressive system, consisting of six rotating 20mm barrels controlled electronically, can fire 3000 heavy-metal-penetrating rounds per minute against missiles penetrating air defenses.

Navy ships are always prepared for action: The Vulcan Phalanx close-in weapons sytem (CIWS)—known as 'sea whiz'—is potent against aircraft *(left);* **taking sextant readings on the port bridge** *(above);* **the destroyer USS** *Fife* **(DD 991) under way off the starboard side of the battleship USS** *New Jersey* **(BB 62)** *(below).*

CRUISERS

The Navy has 30 cruisers in its fleet, ranging greatly in age, size and capability. The oldest, the nine cruisers of the *Leahy* class (CG 16), displacing just over 8200 tons at full load, were originally classed as frigates, but have since been rated as guided-missile cruisers (designated CG). All nine were constructed between 1959 and 1964, but were modernized in the late 1960s and early 1970s. They were conceived and built during a period when the Navy had abandoned the gun in favor of the missile. Surface-to-air missile launchers were placed fore and aft, with an 8-tube launcher as the main antisubmarine weapon. These ships have since been

The USS *Leahy* (CG 16) *(above)*, one of the oldest cruisers, is armed with Harpoon and Standard missiles, two Phalanx close-in weapons sytems and two triple torpedo tubes. The USS *Ticonderoga* (CG 47) *(right)*, one of the newest cruisers, is fitted with the Aegis air defense system which can control as many as 18 Standard missiles simultaneously.

refitted with Harpoon and Standard missiles, as well as the Phalanx. They have a ship's complement of 377 men.

Ten conventionally powered ships were originally scheduled in this class, but one was constructed with a nuclear power plant. This is the USS *Bainbridge* (CGN 25), constructed along the same lines as the *Leahy* class, but with a wider hull to handle nuclear reactors. She also is heavier, displacing 8600 tons at full load.

The last conventionally powered warships of their size to be constructed are the *Belknap*-class (CG 26) cruisers, displacing 8200 tons at full load. They have a complement of 418 men. They are antiaircraft and antisubmarine escorts for the carriers, and they were developed from the smaller *Leahys*. When these ships were constructed between 1962 and 1967, the Navy had changed its thinking on putting guns on board. They are

armed with a single 5-inch 54-caliber gun on the aft deck in addition to its missiles and Phalanx. As in the case of the *Leahys*, 10 ships were planned, but Congress insisted a single ship be built with nuclear propulsion. This is the USS *Truxton* (CGN 35), commissioned in 1967. Like her older half-sisters, she is slightly larger to accommodate her two nuclear reactors. She displaces 9127 tons at full load and carries a ship's crew of 498 men. Her

single 5-inch gun is located on the fore deck rather than the aft deck.

The USS *Long Beach* (CGN 9), displacing 17,525 tons, represents two firsts. She was the first of the smaller surface ships to be powered by a nuclear reactor when she was completed in 1961 and the first to depend completely on missiles rather than guns for defense. However, she has since been refitted with two 5-inch guns on her aft superstructure for

defense against low-flying aircraft and low-profile patrol boats. She is also the heaviest cruiser in the fleet, displacing 17,525 tons. She carries a ship's complement of 1160 men.

The two cruisers of the *California* class (CGN 36), both displacing 10,150 tons with a full load, are more fully developed versions of the USS *Bainbridge* (CGN 25) and the USS *Truxton* (CGN 35), but are larger and more advanced. They were funded and built

Left: The nuclear-powered USS *Truxton* (CGN 35) is armed with Harpoon and Standard missiles, antisubmarine rockets, one 5-inch/54-caliber gun and four fixed torpedo tubes.

Below: The USS *Leahy* (CG 16) and other cruisers in its class originally were classed frigates but underwent extensive modernization between 1967-72.

to take advantage of the nuclear-powered carriers. The carriers are worthless without escorts that also can steam for long distances at high speeds without refueling. The two ships carry a crew of 563 men. They are armed with Harpoon and Standard missiles, as well as antisubmarine rockets, two 5-inch guns, six triple torpedo tubes and two Phalanx systems. The Standard missile is a family of missiles designed to be used against ships, aircraft and in-coming missiles. They have a range of about 10 nautical miles.

The four nuclear-powered cruisers of the *Virginia* class (CGN 38) resemble their older half-sisters in the *California* class. They do not have launchers for antisubmarine warfare, which enabled designers to trim 16 feet of hull length from the ships. However, they are armed with multipurpose rocket launchers and triple torpedo tubes fore and aft. Because of Congressional opposition, the *Virginias* will probably be the last nuclear-powered surface ships constructed unless the cost of this technology drops dramatically. However, with its small group of nuclear cruisers in hand, the Navy can deploy a nuclear-powered carrier task force with unlimited cruising range.

The newest cruisers, the three ships of the *Ticonderoga* class (CB 47), are the most advanced in terms of their fighting capabilities. Their sophisticated Aegis surface-to-air defense system gives them an extremely accurate and reliable defense against missiles launched by other ships, submarines, or airplanes. Aegis was designed and developed to integrate electronic detection with the ship's combat missiles. During deployment off the coast of Lebanon in late 1983, the USS *Ticonderoga* detected friendly aircraft in the area, but maintained surveillance, detection and tracking of enemy aircraft. Eleven are to be constructed in this class, which displace 9600 tons with full load. They are powered by four large gas turbines. Each ship has a complement of 360 men.

DESTROYERS

Because US navy ships now carry computers, large and sophisticated radars, large sonars and missile systems, they are larger than ever before. Most classes of Navy ships have doubled in size since World War II.

The *Spruance*-class destroyer USS *Fletcher* (DD 992) dwarfs the two frigates next to it—the USS *McInerney* (FFG 8) and the USS *Marvin Shields* (FF 1066)—yet its ship's complement of 296 men is within 65 men of either of the smaller vessels.

162

Above: The *Virginia*-class guided missile cruiser USS *Arkansas* (CGN 41) will probably be one of the last nuclear-powered surface ships constructed for the Navy unless the cost of the technology drops to the point where Congress will once more give approval for their building.

Below: The *Charles F Adams*-class guided-missile destroyer USS *Cochrane* (DDG 21), among the oldest destroyers in the fleet, is used primarily for escort duty.

This is especially true of US Navy destroyers. The *Arleigh Burke* (DDG 51) class of destroyers, which will soon go into production, will be the same size as, yet far exceed the fire power of, a World War II cruiser. Despite this increase, it will carry a crew of just 300 men—one-third of those required in the cruiser. Similar manpower savings are evident in the advanced *Spruance-* and *Kidd*-class destroyers and *Oliver Hazard Perry*-class frigates. Manpower reduction has enabled the Navy to operate more efficiently—manpower now represents 30 percent of the 1986 budget compared to 42 percent in 1974. The *Arleigh Burke* class, named after former Chief of Naval Operations Admiral Arleigh Burke of World War II destroyer fame, is designed to replace the *Leahy* and *Belknap* classes of cruisers and the *Farragut* class of guided-missile destroyers. They will be equipped with Aegis, as well as a system to protect their crews against fallout from nuclear, biological and chemical warfare. They are also being constructed with armor and other protection to survive damaging attacks.

The 32 destroyers of the *Spruance* class (DDG 963) were hurriedly constructed to replace a generation of aging World War II-era destroyers that had to be retired in the early 1970s. They are fitted with Harpoon and NATO Sea Sparrow missiles, antisubmarine rockets, two Phalanx systems, two five-inch caliber guns, and two triple torpedo tubes. The first American warships to be powered by gas turbines, they were designed primarily for antisubmarine warfare. They are larger than traditional destroyer designs, displacing 7810 tons. They are also lightly armed, so that they could be constructed rapidly in the large numbers needed by the Navy. The destroyers' lack of weaponry has been widely criticized among Navy personnel, but the modular, rectangular construction of the superstructure will permit new weapons to be installed easily.

The four ships of the *Kidd* class (DDG 993) are closely related to the ships of the *Spruance* class. Displacing 8300 tons and carrying a complement of 338 men, these ships were ordered by the Shah of Iran. The ships were fitted with guided missiles for antiair warfare, a capability not added to the *Spruances*. When the Shah's government fell in 1979, the US Navy took over and completed the ships. However, no more will be added because of their high cost.

The *Charles F Adams* class (DDG 2) of guided-missile destroyers are among the oldest destroyers in the fleet. Constructed between 1958 and 1964, they are updated versions of the now retired *Forrest Sherman*-class designs produced in the postwar period of the 1940s. They displace a modest 4500 tons at full load, and they are used primarily for escort duty. They have a complement of 354 men. There are ten ships in the *Farragut* class (DDG 37), the first ships designed and constructed to carry missiles. They were originally rated as frigates, displace 5300 tons, and carry a crew of 377 men.

It is worth noting that many of the larger surface ships carry helicopters for defensive and tactical purposes. The Navy is now using the SH-2 Seasprite for ASW and antiship and missile operations. The Navy's newest helicopter, the SH-60B Seahawk, better known as the LAMPS (Light Airborne Multipurpose Systems) MkIII helicopter, will soon be deployed aboard most guided-missile destroyers and frigates. The primary mission of this helicopter is to conduct antisubmarine warfare, ship surveillance and targeting, as well as search-and-rescue and medical evacuation. The USS *Underwood* (FFG 36) was the first ship equipped with a production model LAMPS MkIII.

FRIGATES

More than 100 frigates are part of the fleet. Although they provide good protection with their Harpoon and Standard missiles, they remain basically escorts rather than multipurpose warships. The newest frigates, the ships of the *Oliver Hazard Perry* class (FFG 7), represent one of the Navy's best-managed ship-building programs in terms of production and costs. Despite this, the Navy is not seeking more ships in this class because of their limited range and fighting capabilities. Of the 60 planned, only 50 will be constructed. They displace 3585 tons at full load. They are designed to use far fewer men than their older predecessors, the

Opposite: Two views of the USS *Elliott* (DD 967) whose primary mission is anti-submarine warfare (ASW). The basic hull design of *Spruance*-class destroyers provides an unusual potential for growth as improved weapons and electronics systems are developed.

Below: Another *Spruance*-class destroyer, the USS *Fletcher* (DD 992), fires a Harpoon antiship missile.

The *Oliver Hazard Perry*-class guided missile frigate USS *Sides* (FFG 14) is nudged into port by the harbor tug during San Francisco's 1984 Fleet Week Celebration. San Francisco is a long-time Navy town that enthusiastically supports the annual Fleet Week festivities. In the background is the USS *Fletcher* (DD 992).

Knox class (FF 1052), with a ship's complement of 231, including air crew. Although featuring similar layouts with a single hull and shaft, they are powered by two gas turbines that allow them to continue to operate even if one breaks down. They displace 3585 tons.

The *Knox*-class of frigates, the second generation of postwar escort warships, is the largest class of Navy ships constructed since 1945. Forty-six were built in the period between 1965 and 1974, with a single engine and single shaft to make them cheaper. Displacement ranges from 3877 tons full load to 4200 tons full load. Other frigate classes include the *Garcia* (FF 1040), *Bronstein* (FF 1037), *Brooke* (FF 1), and *Glover* (FF 1098) classes. They are of similar size and capabilities.

SUBMARINES

The Navy's fleet of submarines are divided into classes: nuclear-powered ballistic-missile submarines (SSBN) and nuclear attack submarines (SSN). The largest of the SSBNs are the submarines of the *Ohio* class. They displace 18,700 tons, with a length of 560 feet and a beam of 42 feet. Older ships in the SSBN fleet include the older ships of the *Ethan Allen* class, which displace 7880 tons. The submarines of the *Ohio* class carry Trident missiles and four torpedo tubes. They carry a complement of 133 men. Five have been constructed and four more are on order. Even more are expected to be built in the years ahead, despite ongoing opposition from polit-

Above: **The USS *Meyerkord* (FF 1058) and the USS *New Jersey* (BB 62).**

Below: **The missile compartment of the USS *Ohio* (SSBN 726), the first Trident.**

Right: **The USS *Michigan* (SSBN 727), another Trident-armed 'boomer.'**

ical opponents within and without the US government. The Trident, a three-staged, solid-fuel rocket, has a range of 4000 nautical miles. It carries thermonuclear Multiple Independently Targetable Re-entry Vehicles (MIRVs) capable of delivering several warheads on individual targets.

Continued on page 74

The launching of the USS *Portsmouth* (SSN 707), one of the *Los Angeles*-class attack submarines yet being produced. Its armament includes Harpoon and Tomahawk missiles, SUBROC, Mk 48 torpedoes and four torpedo tubes. The partially complete USS *Rhode Island* submarine is seen in the background.

Maintenance crew aboard the USS *Enterprise* (CVN 65) ready an F-14 from VF-1, the 'Wolfpack' squadron. In the background is the colorfully marked tail of an F-14 from VF-2, the 'Bounty Hunters' squadron. At the time of this photograph, the two squadrons formed the carrier air wing that deployed to sea together.

The US Navy pioneered nuclear propulsion and submarine warfare in constructing the famed USS *Nautilus* and then experimented with a number of different designs in the hull and nuclear power plants before moving ahead with acceptable designs. *Permit*-class submarines, built in the 1960s, were the first constructed in sizeable numbers and 13 remain in commission. They have been joined by the 20 submarines in the *Sturgeon* class and 37 submarines in the *Los Angeles* class. These two classes are designed to hunt submarines and to protect the SSBNs from underwater attack. They are armed with the Sub-Harpoon and submarine-launched cruise missile systems, as well as conventional and wire-guided torpedoes. Since submarines are tracked by the noise they emit underwater, the two classes are fitted with two contra-rotating propellers on the same shaft to reduce propulsion noise. As a result, these operate more quietly than their Russian counterparts. The Navy is seeking to construct 18 more in the *Los Angeles* class through the end of the

Pegasus-class hydrofoils: USS *Taurus* (PHM 3) *(below right)*; USS *Aguila* (PHM 4) *(bottom left)*; and USS *Pegasus* (PHM 1) on night attack *(overleaf)*. All have speeds of 48 knots when foilborne and a range of over 1200 miles if hullborne— mighty impressive but mighty expensive.

decade. The *Los Angeles*-class subs are 360 feet long and displace 6900 tons. They carry a crew of 127 men. The *Sturgeons* are 292 feet long and displace 4640 tons. They carry a ship's crew of 142.

The two classes are armed with Harpoon and Tomahawk missiles, plus torpedoes. The Mark 48 torpedo, a wire-guided torpedo said to be the most complex torpedo ever developed, is carried by all US Navy submarines. More than 3000 have been delivered. It is about 19 feet long and weighs 3500 lb. It has a range of 23 miles.

OTHER WARSHIPS

One of the more interesting of the smaller warships of the US Navy is one of the most controversial—the *Pegasus* (PHM) class of hydrofoils.

The USS *Cayuga* (LST 1186) whose design is a radical departure from earlier amphibious tank-landing ships. Its 35-ton bow ramp can be lowered onto the beach or married to a causeway to allow rapid unloading of vehicles and equipment. Another ramp extending from the tank deck provides rapid vehicle access to the main deck and bow ramp. Its stern gate provides for the launching and retrieval of amphibious vehicles.

Ships of this class displace just 221 tons at full load and ride above the surface of the water at 48 knots full speed. Six are operating in the Key West area off the coast of Florida. Originally conceived as a NATO ship to be constructed jointly by Germany, Italy and the United States, only six were built. The two European countries withdrew from the project. The ships are armed with eight Harpoon missiles and one 76mm gun. This is an impressive fit of heavy armament on

Opposite and left: The scissors on the front of the USS *Cayuga* (LST 1186) hoist up the landing ramp and a detail of its control house on top of the bridge. (The bumper sticker on the control house reminds us that not all the creatures with whom the *Cayuga* shares the sea are made of steel.) In the background *(opposite)* is the general-purpose amphibious-assault ship USS *Peleliu* (LHA 5) that can carry a complete Marine Battalion Landing Team, their supplies and equipment.

Below: Ammunition ship USS *Haleakala* (AE 25) displaces 15.5 to 16 tons.

an extremely fast and maneuverable hull, but the hydrofoils are very expensive to build for their size and range.

The *Iwo Jima, Tarawa* and *Wasp* classes of amphibious-assault ships (LHD, LHA, LPH) represent the Navy's vital and important relationship to the Marine Corps. These ships provide the Marines a viable means of getting from ship to shore by helicopter to augment movement of other troops and equipment by landing craft. The USS *Iwo Jima* (LPH 2) was the first ship designed and constructed to operate helicopters. Each ship can carry a Marine battalion landing team, as well as its weapons and equipment and various support personnel. The USS *Guam* (LPH 9) has operated the Harrier AV-8A V/STOL (Vertical/Short Take-Off and Landing) from its decks. Ships in the *Iwo Jima* class displace 18,000 tons at full load, and the hangar deck can accommodate 20 CH-46 Sea Knight or 11 CH-53 Sea Stallion helicopters.

Austin-class amphibious transport docks such as the USS *Dubuque* (LPD 8) *(right)* and the USS *Denver* (LPD 9) *(below)* can carry 900 troops, up to six CH-46 Sea Knight helicopters and from 4 to 20 landingcraft depending on type.

THE UNITED STATES NAVY IN ACTION

Although the ships of the US Navy have been designed and deployed to counter the threat of the Soviet navy, a major confrontation has never come about. Instead, the Navy has been called upon to safeguard US interests around the globe, especially in troubled hotspots such as the Mediterranean and the waters around the oil-producing countries of the Middle East.

Carriers, though armed with the most powerful weapons of the fleet, often take the backseat to other ships when the Navy is called upon to carry out military assignments. The Navy reactivated the *Iowa*-class battleships so that it could have immense weaponry to deal with an increasingly hostile political and social climate. The Navy realized that these large, powerful warships could serve as showpieces of renewed US determination to maintain its political strength throughout the world.

The decade of the 1980s has been one of flexibility and change for the US Navy as it has been called upon to respond to fast-moving political and hostile conditions around the globe. It has been able to respond with surprising success close to home, as well as in

Opposite: **The battleship USS *New Jersey* (BB 62) captured on film by ship's photographer PH2 Rick Sforza as it cuts loose with a nine-gun full broadside salvo. Somewhere nine tons of steel will rain down on a target.**

Above: **The breech of one of the *New Jersey's* big 16-inch guns.**

distant oceans. For example, it was ordered to assist other US Military forces in the waters of the Caribbean in 1983. While steaming toward the Mediterranean to hold exercises, a naval battle group consisting of the USS *Independence*, her escorts and an accompanying Marine Amphibious Ready Group (MARG) were suddenly ordered to assist in the Grenada rescue mission. The Navy played a key role in the invasion of the island and the rescue of American students studying medicine there.

Just eight days later, the same force was directed to the waters off Beirut to conduct reconnaissance flights in the mountains above Beirut at the request of the government of Lebanon. The highlands sheltered guns that were raining fire down on the city. Fighters of the *Independence*, assisted by the large 16-inch guns of the USS *New Jersey*, bombed and shelled suspected terrorist positions. The *New Jersey* was joined by the cruisers USS *Ticonderoga* and USS *Virginia* with their 5-inch guns. The same MARG that had participated in the Grenada operation helped to evacuate 1000 noncombatant Americans and foreign nationals from Lebanese ports using Marine

helicopters and Navy landing craft. The evacuees were then transported by ship to Cyprus.

In the waters of the Red Sea, the surveying ship USS *Harkness* and the amphibious dock-landing ship USS *Shreveport* with her RH-53 mine-clearing helicopters were sent to locate and destroy mines damaging international ships approaching the Suez Canal. Another contingent of RH-53 helicopters, as well as the flagship of the commander of the Middle East, the USS *LaSalle* (AGF 3), were ordered to the area to support the efforts and keep shipping lanes open.

A Navy battle group consisting of destroyers, frigates and submarines has remained stationed in the northern Arabian Sea to monitor on-going hostilities between Iran and Iraq. This force remains on station to protect allied sea lanes and to provide an air warning and defense screen to US-flag tankers under charter to the Military Sealift Command (MSC). The ships steamed to the region after 60 vessels, mostly oil tankers, were hit by aircraft fire between March and December

1984. The tactics were not like those conducted during convoys across the Atlantic. The warships established a radar screen from the Strait of Hormuz in Bahrain to the Persian Gulf. This task group has enabled the Navy to protect its oil shipments to the island of Diego Garcia in the Indian Ocean and the US naval base at Subic Bay in the Philippines.

The shipping lanes through the Indian Ocean are among the world's most critical. Because of this, the Navy now maintains a continual presence in the region. During 1984, the air

The USS *New Jersey's* 16-inch guns fire off the coast of Lebanon *(above)*; a sailor has his finger on the trigger of the gun inside turret one *(left)*.

***Opposite top:* Indian Ocean Task Force under way during the Iran hostage crisis *(from front to back)*: carriers USS *Kitty Hawk* (CV 63), USS *Midway* (CV 41) and USS *Nimitz* (CVN 68) with escorts.**

***Opposite bottom:* A crewman aboard the USS *Nimitz* (CVN 68) wears a cold weather face mask during 'Fleetex 82,' a CINCPAC exercise for the US Navy, Air Force, Coast Guard and Canadian Navy.**

craft carrier USS *Ranger* and her battle group operated in this region and set a record for continuous operations for a conventionally powered carrier battle group. They remained at sea for 121 days and steamed more than 50,000 miles. During the course of this deployment, the Navy concluded the first visit to an Indian port by a US naval warship in 13 years.

It was recognized in the late 1970s that the Military Sealift Command could not adequately respond to emergencies, especially in distant places like the Indian Ocean. Recognizing the

lack of sealift capability, the Carter administration ordered the Navy to preposition a small force of ships and supplies at Diego Garcia. Owned by Great Britain, the island had already been used as a base for some years on a small scale by the US. The prepositioned force consists of 17 ships, including a water tanker, ammunition ship and cargo ships of various types. They have been given the designation of the Near-Term Preposition Force (NTPF), and are loaded with petroleum, oil and lubricants, as well as water. Four are designed to carry vehicles and one carries a hospital designed for 500 men. They can sustain a Marine force of 12,500 men for 30 days. One third of the force is under way at all times, and all ships get under way every three months and participate in convoy exercises. Fifteen of the ships are chartered, while two are owned by the government. They are maintained in such a state of readiness that they can get under way in two hours when in port.

The Navy also maintains visibility in the waters off the coast of Central

America, where it monitors arms shipments from the Soviet Bloc to countries such as Cuba and Nicaragua. The fleet has conducted numerous exercises there to demonstrate US resolve to support neighbors and allies against Communist insurgency movements.

US Navy ships have also been used to help obstruct the flow of illegal drugs into the United States. Navy support of a major US Coast Guard drug-interdiction operation in the Caribbean Sea in 1983 resulted in the seizure of 24 vessels carrying illegal drugs.

On the moonless night of 10 October 1985, high over the eastern Mediterranean Sea, six US Navy F-14 Tomcats launched from the USS *Saratoga* intercepted, then forced down, an

The ever-vigilant Navy: A carrier crewman *(top)* signals to the guided-missile frigate cruising alongside; pilots of the SH-60 Sea Hawks *(above)* patrol for hostile submarines; and F-14s set out on a sunset mission *(opposite)*.

Egyptian Boeing 737 at a NATO base near Sigonella on the island of Sicily. They had been ordered aloft by the direct orders of President Ronald Reagan. The 737 carried four members of the Palestinian Liberation Organization who had hijacked an Italian cruise ship, the *Achille Lauro*. For two days, they had held 500 passengers hostage including dozens of Americans. They murdered a 69-year-old handicapped US citizen and threw his body overboard along with his wheelchair.

The orders to intercept came while the USS *Saratoga* was steaming northwest in the waters of the Adriatic Sea near the coast of Albania. She turned south and prepared to launch the six planes, which were sent aloft with two E-2C radar planes and two air tankers for refueling.

Just after midnight, the Tomcats spotted the 737 near the island of Crete after it had lifted off from Egypt. It was a difficult mission to spot the 737 in the crowded skies above the Mediterranean, but US officials credited a steady flow of accurate intelligence for the Navy's ability to single out the plane from the other commercial jets.

The Navy F-14s had been launched even before the 737 had left a military base outside Cairo and were waiting over Crete. They shadowed the plane while it was denied permission to land in Tunis, Tunisia and Athens, Greece. Then they surrounded the aircraft on four sides and signaled it to land in Sicily, with the permission of the Italian government.

The pilot of the 737, who was in radio contact with the US Navy fighters, agreed to land in Sicily. No shots were fired. When the plane touched down, it was greeted by specially trained US troops who were at the base. The four terrorists were arrested by Italian officials, along with the Egyptian crew of the plane.

It was an unusual assignment for

The USS *Kitty Hawk* (CV 63) enters San Francisco Bay with
Coast Guard escort for Fleet Week 83 *(below)*. A crewman mans
the helm of the *Kitty Hawk (opposite top)* which displaces
80,800 tons fully loaded and carries about 95 aircraft.

The rallying call of the Navy bugleman has sounded for over two centuries. Today's Navy remains committed to the Navy's founding purpose—guarding the maritime interests of the United States by keeping the sea lanes open.

the Navy and its aviators, but it was one carried out quietly and successfully. It was a mission that showed the daring and flexibility of the US Navy.

THE UNITED STATES NAVY TODAY

Today's US Navy is an ever-changing naval force on the world's oceans. When it was created more than 200 years ago, it was designed to protect US maritime interests not only close to home but on the high seas far from home. That mission remains as true today as it did during the period of the Revolutionary War. It is a naval force in transition, with several new ships of advanced design and weaponry joining the fleet and veteran ships departing for the scrap yard as they come to the end of their service lives.

The Navy today is under challenge and test, especially from its shadowy and threatening opponent, the Soviet navy. In recent years, ships of the Soviet fleet have been deployed nearly everywhere on the globe, including the waters of the Western Hemisphere where the threat has moved very close to home for the US. Off the coast of Central America, the Soviet Union has sent numerous task-force fleets consisting of guided missile helicopter cruisers and destroyers.

As the Soviets have increased the size of their navy, they have been more willing to embark on military adventures far from their homeland. It is now a navy designed for offensive action—to cut off the free flow of trade and commerce in the event of war. The US remains a naval power by necessity, dependent upon imports of goods and strategic materials vital to its economy. The seas are the lifeblood of the United States. It is for this reason that the modern Navy has been designed to keep these sea lanes open.

The Navy remains an ever-vigilant force. It must be prepared to venture into harm's way when necessary and control the seas to assure access for the United States and its allies. In the words of US Secretary of Defense Caspar Weinberger: 'We know that strength alone is not enough, but without it there can be no effective diplomacy and peace. Conversely, weakness and hopeful passivity are only self-defeating. They invite the very aggression and instability they would seek to avoid.'

Below: The *Virginia*-class guided missile cruiser USS *Arkansas* (CGN 41) in San Francisco Bay.

THE UNITED STATES
MARINES
TODAY

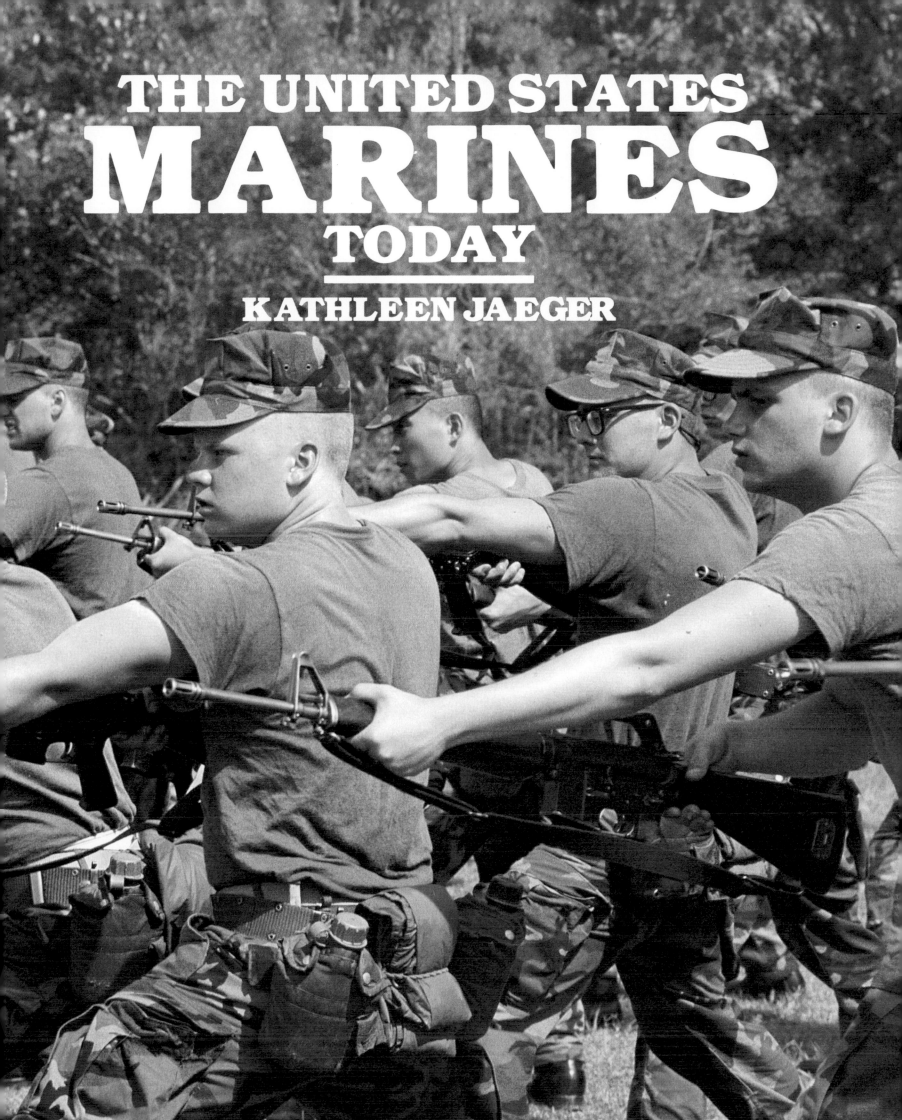

THE UNITED STATES
MARINES
TODAY

KATHLEEN JAEGER

Previous page: Bayonet techniques are part of every male Marine's training.

Below: Recruits practice to achieve the maximum score of 20 on the pull-

INTRODUCTION TO THE UNITED STATES MARINES

The need for both soldiers and sailors to man ships of war is ages old. Great Britain used marines with magnificent success as she set about colonizing the world, and one of those same colonies adopted a force similar to the Royal Navy and used it as a means to win independence from King George III.

The Continental Marines, which developed into the United States Marine Corps, was officially established on 10 November 1775 when Congress passed a resolution providing for two battalions of Marines to include 'good seamen or so acquainted with maritime affairs as to be able to serve with advantage by 'sea when required; that they be enlisted and commissioned to serve for and during the present war between Great Britain and the colonies.'

Recruitment for these first and second battalions went briskly, possibly aided by the fact that the first Marine headquarters was established in a tavern. It was at the Tun Tavern on

Opposite: Marines come ashore (using causeway) at Lebanon in May 1983.

Right: Colors are proudly displayed by recruits at the Parris Island training depot during their graduation ceremony.

King Street in Philadelphia that Samuel Nicholas, the first commandant of Marines, and Robert Mullan, owner of the tavern and a captain in the new corps, set about the task of attracting likely young men with tales of high adventure and rich bounty, all sweetened with 'one on the house.' Whether it was because of the tavern, the tales or a free drink is pure speculation, but it is fact that the nation's first naval expedition sailed on 17 February 1776 with a full complement of 268 Marines.

The Continental Marines participated in virtually all of the naval operations of the Revolutionary War, growing in number to 124 officers and 3000 enlisted men. However, after the Peace of Paris, both the Navy and Marine Corps began to dwindle in size, the latter all but disappearing. It was not until 1798, after American commerce had been plagued by French and Barbary Coast pirates, that the nation again realized its need for the Marines.

Samuel Sewall, chairman of the Congressional Naval Committee, began work on a bill to raise 'a battalion to be called the Marine Corps,' a separate service within the Navy. In July 1798 President John Adams was

Marines remain in a constant state of readiness by regularly training for all types of combat situations. Below they practice their most well known function, taking the beachhead.

Above: **Commandant of Marines Paul X Kelley (right) and President Reagan.**

Opposite and left: **Recruits are lectured on the art of self defense, and boot camp graduates undergo an exhaustive inspection by their commanding officer.**

presented with the bill, which he promptly signed into law. William Ward Burrows was then appointed commandant of the corps. Major Burrows is also remembered today as the commandant responsible for establishing the Marine Corps Band.

The mission of the Corps as described in 1798 was to perform sea duty of an amphibious nature, to serve in forts and garrisons of the United States and most significantly, to perform 'any other duty on shore, as the President, at his discretion shall direct.' The mission of today's Marine Corps has deviated little from this initial prescription, and experience from the Halls of Montezuma to the shelled streets of Beirut has taught Americans that their trust in the Marines is well placed.

The relationship of the Marine Corps to the other services has varied over the years, ranging from a small subordinate of the Navy to its present status as one of four distinct military services within the Department of Defense. Even today this statement causes occasional confusion because though the Department of Defense consists of the three Departments of the Army, Air Force and Navy, these departments are made up of the four distinct services of Army, Air Force, Navy and Marine Corps. The Marine Corps and Navy together make up the Department of the Navy with the commandant of the Marine Corps reporting directly to the secretary of the Navy. The commandant is a member of the Joint Chiefs of Staff, and in that capacity acts as one of the principal military advisors not only to the president, but to the National Security Council and to the secretary of Defense. The current commandant is General Paul X Kelley who took office on 1 July 1983, 28th in a list that includes the names Archibald Henderson and John A Lejuene.

Marines today number almost 200,000, a much smaller number than any of the other three services. How-

ever, the Marines have always professed that the smaller size only serves to prove the elite nature of the Corps. Even the slick recruitment posters advertise for just 'a few good men.' This attitude is as old as the Corps itself and is responsible in no small part for what the Marines call *esprit de corps*, that binding pride that begins in boot camp and is carried throughout a Marine's life.

Though debate over the exact organization of the Corps never seems to end, it is clear that whether in partnership with the Navy or under direct orders from the president, the Marine Corps is the nation's force-in-readiness. This constant state of preparedness is achieved by an organization aimed both at strength and flexi-

bility. The basic combat structure of the Marine Corps consists of the Marine Air-Ground Task Force (MAGTF). There are three types of MAGTFs: the Marine Amphibious Unit (MAU), the Marine Amphibious Brigade (MAB) and the Marine Amphibious Force (MAF). Each may be tailored both in size and configuration to meet a specific operational requirement. They are divided into four elements: the Command Element (CE), the Ground Combat Element

Previous page: **Drill instructors enjoy a rare quiet moment at Parris Island.**

Above: **A MAU Command Post in Lebanon.**

Opposite and right: **Marines train under freezing conditions and a paratrooper makes a reconnaissance drop.**

(GCE), the Aviation Combat Element (ACE) and the Combat Service Support Element (CSSE).

The CE allows a MAGTF to function with the kind of close integration and coordination possible only under a single commander. A MAU is commanded by a colonel, a MAB by a brigadier general and a MAF by a major general or a lieutenant general.

The GCE consists of artillery, tank, amphibious assault vehicle, reconnaissance and combat engineer units. It can range in size from a single infantry battalion to one or more divisions.

The ACE, whether consisting of a single composite helicopter squadron or several Marine Aircraft Wings may include offensive air support or air reconnaissance. An ACE can be equipped for antiair warfare, electronic warfare and to serve as command and control. The close air-ground team relationship this makes possible has always been a Marine Corps trademark.

The CSSE includes both Marine and Navy support elements. It can range in size from a single MAU Service Support Group deployed for a specific and limited mission to a MAF Service Sup-

Left: **Marines hit the beach in Lebanon in 1983.**

Below: **Under a blazing desert sun, a Marine confers with his unit.**

port Group able to provide a total range of logistic support from motor transport to dental services.

All of the above elements come together in varying sizes and configurations to make up the three types of MAGTFs, the smallest and most responsive of which is the MAU, consisting of approximately 2500 personnel. It was this type of force that the Marines deployed to Grenada during Operation *Urgent Fury* in October 1983. Today the United States continuously deploys MAUs in the Mediterranean Sea and western Pacific Ocean, and periodically in the Atlantic and Indian Oceans and the Caribbean Sea. These MAUs, in position and alert, are ready to respond to any international crisis when directed by the National Command Authority.

MAUs are normally sea based and may be deployed by amphibious ships or airlifted for a limited amount of time carrying supplies for approximately 15 days. MAUs often serve as the forward element of a MAB and consist of a Battalion Landing Team (BLT) and Composite Aircraft Squadron. The BLT is

Top: **A Marine AH-1T Cobra gunship is readied for flight.**

Right: **An Amphibious Assault Team during 'Team Spirit 85,' a joint US military forces exercise held in Korea.**

A Marine M60 tank leaves a billowing trail of dust in its wake.

216

reinforced by tank, antiarmor, artillery, reconnaissance, amphibious assault vehicle and combat engineer units. The MAU ACE contains four types of helicopters: CH-46 Sea Knights, CH-53 Sea Stallions, AH-1 Cobras and UH-1 Hueys. The Cobras may be replaced or reinforced by AV-8 Harrier V/STOL (Vertical/Short Takeoff and Landing) attack aircraft as the tactical situation dictates.

MABs are the next largest MAGTFs, consisting of approximately 13,000 personnel. They can be deployed for up to 30 days without resupply, and normally embark aboard as many as 20 Navy amphibious ships. MABS are capable of amphibious operations and subsequent operations ashore. The GCE is a task-organized Regimental Landing Team (RLT) consisting of two to five infantry battalions, an artillery battalion, a tank company and an anti-armor platoon. The ACE is a Marine

Left, top and bottom: US Navy landing ships such as these are used to transport Marine troops, weapons and materiel wherever they are needed.

Below: A Marine jeep unit on patrol.

Right and far right: Troops and their vehicles deploy from helicopters, and Marines in camouflage gear descend into battle, first to fight.

Above: **The pilot of an F/A-18 Hornet attack aircraft prepares for flight.**

Left: **A major general confers with two officers.**

Opposite top left and right: **Marines outfitted in elaborate camouflage gear.**

Opposite, top middle: **The Stinger is a man-portable antiaircraft guided missile.**

Aircraft Group (MAG) and consists of fixed-wing aircraft including AV-8 Harriers, A-4 Skyhawks, F-4 Phantoms, F/A-18 Hornets, A-6 Intruders, OV-10 Broncos and KC-130 Hercules as well as the same types of helicopters used in a MAU.

The MAF is the largest and most powerful of MAGTFs and may range in size from less than one to several divisions and aircraft wings, and include as many as 50,000 personnel. The Marine division is composed of three infantry regiments, an artillery regiment, a tank battalion, an amphibious assault vehicle battalion, a com-

bat engineer battalion and a reconnaissance battalion. The ACE is normally a Marine Aircraft Wing (MAW) which is specifically task organized for the mission. It may include as many as 650 aircraft, both fixed wing and helicopters, plus additional aircraft wings for additional combat power ashore as necessary. The MAW also includes air command and control elements with Hawk, Redeye and Stinger missile launchers.

Though these three types of MAGTFs differ greatly in size and configuration, they are each task organized for rapid deployment as part of the Navy–Marine Corps team. With timely intelligence and early deployment on amphibious ships, they can provide a continuous presence in international waters while remaining independent of established ports and airfields. MAGTFs can build quickly in size, proceed to a crisis area without revealing their exact destination and project a

selected degree of self-supporting combat power ashore. They are able to avoid the necessity to negotiate staging, transit, overflight or base rights, rent or positioning of supplies and can be rapidly withdrawn after operations, providing NCA with positive control over the level and duration of the commitment.

The organization of the MAGTFs allows for flexibility in strength, mobility and size, each of which can be precisely tailored to the specific mission assignment and assessed capability of the opposing forces. MAGTFs can operate equally well as a naval force; part of a joint task force with the Army, Navy and Air Force; as a separate service; as a combined task force with US allies; or as a joint combined task force of US forces and allies. Combined with the ability to be deployed by sealift or airlift, Marines are able to go anywhere America or her interests are endangered, quickly and efficiently.

BECOMING A UNITED STATES MARINE

Every future enlisted US Marine, whether aspiring to someday pilot an F/A-18 or guard the US embassy in Cairo, begins at the same place —the recruit depot. It is here, within minutes of debarking from the bus, that boot camp begins. Frequently described as probably the most difficult challenge a person can face short of combat, the regimen of boot camp has been successfully completed by more than half a million Americans over the past 10 years. It is extremely difficult precisely because the men who survive it may one day face combat.

The Marine Corps has two recruit training depots, one at San Diego, California and the other at Parris Island, South Carolina. Women recruits are trained only by Parris Island's Woman Recruit Training Command. Their program differs in some respects from that of the male recruits; however, the goal is the same: to build basic Marines.

Boot camp is a time of physically, mentally and psychologically demanding training. It begins with an initial period of receiving and processing. Within hours of arriving at the depot the recruit has received an introductory lecture on the Uniform Code of Military

Opposite: **A Marine recruit gives his all on the basic training circuit course.**

Above: **A recruit demonstrates the arduous skill of rappelling.**

Justice, an issue of camouflage utilities, combat boots and underwear, and for men, their first Marine Corps haircut. The close-cropped haircut endured by recruits has over the years become a symbol worn proudly by the Marine Security Guard battalion serving in embassies around the world. Recently, however, the extremely recognizable haircut is being re-evaluated for security reasons, as worldwide terrorist attacks necessitate a lower-visibility approach.

Initial processing begins with a 'contraband check.' Knives, candy, gum, radios and anything else the recruit will not need during training is tagged and put away for safekeeping. The actual processing lasts six days and consists of interviews, lectures, testing and drill. This receiving and processing stage, an intentionally low-stress period, gives way to the actual training procedure.

Marine recruit training is divided into three phases. Phase one includes the basic information and training necessary for the individual to function as a Marine and for the platoon to function as an efficient and cohesive team. It begins with an introduction to physical conditioning, close order

Above: A DI addresses his recruits.

Left and bottom: During the processing stage, newly shaven recruits are issued equipment and later take placement exams.

drill, first aid, guard duty, personal hygiene, the M16 rifle, military courtesy and discipline and Marine Corps history, customs and traditions.

Combat effectiveness depends to a great extent on the physical condition of the troops. This first phase devotes many hours to physical testing and conditioning in preparation for the physical fitness test (PFT) administered during the final training phase. By the end of phase one the platoon is beginning to look like and function as a team.

The second phase of training is dedicated to the mastery of marksmanship. The initial period is spent learning safety procedures and elementary firing techniques. Later, instructors work with members of the platoon individually to perfect firing techniques and to correct deficiencies. At the end of this training the recruits fire for record and are presented with marksmanship badges by the drill instructors. The end of phase two is called Service Week and is spent in 'mess duty' and other activities aimed at maintaining the recruit depot in a proper state of cleanliness.

Above: Close combat training includes man-to-man sessions employing the pugil stick.

Below: A recruit eyes her goal: the top of the rope.

Below: A determined recruit battles an obstacle course.

Overleaf: The circuit course is one of four rigorous courses specially designed to get recruits into prime physical condition.

Above and left: A recruit's M16 receives a thorough inspection, and an instructor offers advice during rifle training.

Opposite: M16 training, and a recruit clutches his rifle as he dodges simulated gunfire during field training.

Phase three consists of field training, the physical fitness test and the battalion commander's inspection. Field training includes offensive and defensive combat techniques, including night and day movements, field fire, as well as amphibious and helicopter assault doctrine. Since women are forbidden by law to engage in combat, they spend this time studying combat support and defensive techniques. However, weapons training is conducted.

The physical fitness test is the culmination of the intensive physical training and conditioning of boot camp. To prepare for the test, recruits run up to three miles a day, climb rope to develop arm and shoulder strength, and run a course consisting of 12 obstacles in progressive degrees of difficulty.

Marines are recognized worldwide as much by their outstanding appearance as by their fighting ability. Accordingly, one of the last hurdles a recruit must clear is the battalion commander's inspection. In preparation for this event recruits undergo meticulous uniform fittings. Equipment is examined and re-examined. Rifles,

228

Above: **Recruits attempt the infiltration course in a simulated combat situation.**

Left: **A dripping recruit completes a portion of the confidence course.**

slings and belts are spotless, shoes are polished and brass is shining. After passing the battalion commander's inspection, the physical fitness test and the final drill evaluation, the recruit is ready for graduation.

It is on graduation day that the recruit is addressed for the first time by the title he or she has earned — 'Marine.' After some of the toughest and most demanding training in the world, they are Marines. The Marine emblem 'Eagle, Globe and Anchor' is a part of their uniform and the Marine motto, *Semper Fidelis* (Always Faithful), a part of their lives.

After successfully completing boot camp the new Marine is ready to enter a job skill training program based on both the individual's interests and abilities as well as the needs of the Marine Corps. The program consists of formal training at Marine Corps or other service schools and on-the-job

Above: **Simulated nighttime combat comes as close as possible to the real thing.**

Right: **Four obstacle courses test the mettle of prospective Marines.**

training, and may last anywhere from a month to more than a year. Currently more than 75 percent of new Marines attend a formal school after boot camp. Available occupations range from aircraft maintenance to weather surveillance and all but those that are combat related are open to both men and women. In addition to formal training for their specific occupation, Marines are also encouraged to further their education. To this end the Marine Corps offers off-duty education programs as basic as completing a high school diploma or as complex as earning a doctorate degree. The Marine Corps will pay from 75–90 percent of tuition costs, depending on the individual's rank and time in service, and offers many financial aid programs. These policies serve to benefit the individual Marine by improving career opportunities, and the Corps by constantly upgrading the caliber of personnel.

Rappelling is only one of many skills mastered by recruits during the final and most demanding phase of basic.

Opposite and below: Graduation day. The spirit, pride and discipline these Marines acquired during the rigors of boot camp will remain with them always.

WOMEN MARINES

It would be impossible to tell the story of today's Marines without discussing the increasingly important role of the woman Marine. Walking the fine line between awareness of women's rights and traditional military thinking has not been easy for any of the services. The Marine Corps has long realized the advantage of recruiting women for service and continues to benefit from this policy.

The Marine Corps first enlisted women during World War I to perform clerical tasks and free the men in those assignments for combat duty. Opha Mae Johnson, the forerunner of today's women Marines, enlisted on 13 August 1918, just one day after the secretary of the Navy authorized the Navy and Marine Corps to accept women for service. A total of 305 women served briefly but efficiently during the war, but by 1922 all Women Reservists had returned to civilian life and the Marine Corps was again strictly a man's world.

World War II saw formation of the United States Marine Corps Women's Reserve with a recruitment slogan of 'Free a Marine to Fight,' and though

After arduous training that includes rappelling *(opposite above)*, graduation ceremonies for women Marines are particularly meaningful *(left and opposite bottom)*. The captain at work *(below)* is one of over 9300 women serving in Marine noncombatant roles.

Many recruits are surprised at the amounts of strength and stamina required to qualify in the use of the M16A2 rifle.

Top left: **A recruit in one of the four rifle firing positions.**

Middle and bottom left: **Recruits are tested on their use of the gas mask.**

met with skepticism on high at the beginning, hard work by both men and women eventually made the program a success. With a peak strength of over 19,000, almost the size of a Marine Corps division, the women reserves were told by General Alexander A Vandegrift that they could 'feel responsible for putting the 6th Marine Division in the field, for without the women filling jobs throughout the Marine Corps there would not have been sufficient men available to form that division.'

Though the line of women in the Marine Corps has been unbroken since 1942, attitudes about how they

Above: **One of the goals of the circuit course is to build upper body strength.**

Right: **A lone recruit cools down after running a demanding obstacle course.**

best serve the military mission have changed over the years and are still evolving. Today's woman Marine is assured the opportunity to advance in her career as far as her abilities will take her. A recent Woman Marine Review was conducted by the Corps to deal with questions applying specifically to the classification, assignment and deployment of enlisted women Marines. The review was convened with four objectives: to ensure commanders have sufficient men for deployment requirements; to control the combat risk for women; to guarantee equitable opportunity for men and women to serve in the Fleet Marine

Clockwise from left: **Female recruits in formation on the challenge course; in nuclear, biological and chemical warfare training and during the emblem ceremony.**

Force and the supporting establishment; and to ensure fair and equitable career progression for all Marines. Each of these objectives was dealt with and the resulting Marine Corps Order 1300.8M, published in March 1985, defines the role of enlisted women in today's Marine Corps.

One of the most striking changes concerning the role of women in the Marine Corps has to do with combat training. Beginning in October of 1985

women began studying combat techniques in response to an order by Commandant Kelley. Though women will still be excluded from units likely to engage in combat, it is felt that because of the unpredictable nature of conflicts in today's world, women may find themselves in combat situations and must be trained to protect themselves and their positions.

Combat training will consist of qualifying in the use of the M16 rifle, fighting techniques including cover, concealment and camouflage as well as how to handle grenades, mines and booby traps. Women will receive addi-

tional training in nuclear, biological and chemical defenses and the use of deadly force as a part of guard duty.

Because women will not be assigned to combat duty or to any unit likely to engage in combat, they will not be trained in offensive techniques such as the use of bayonets, combat formations, offensive techniques of fire, ship to shore movement, day or night offensive operations, patrols and ambushes and rubber boat training.

Today's woman Marine will be prepared to protect herself and her position in the event of unexpected enemy fire or terrorist attack.

UNITED STATES MARINES IN ACTION

The strength and security of the United States in today's international climate depends not only upon the ability to protect her shores but also to project a visible strength across the seas to any who would doubt her resolve. During wartime the mission is clear and the Marines are there, 'first to fight' to protect America's interests. During peacetime the mission is often less defined, yet the Marines remain stationed around the world in any potentially volatile area, using their visible strength as a deterrent while remaining ready to take any action required. In this capacity Marines have served in operations that have provided the satisfaction of a 'mission accomplished' as in Grenada and those providing only the painful frustration of undefined conflict as in Beirut.

The Marine Corps' most recent involvement in Beirut began on 25 August 1982 when 800 Marines became part of a multinational peace-keeping force with France and Italy. The force had been established to aid in the withdrawal of Israeli forces from Beirut and the evacuation of Palestine Liberation Organization (PLO) and Syrian forces. It was hoped that this

Opposite: Marine tanks in camouflage paint schemes on desert maneuvers.

Above: A Marine at his post in Lebanon in 1983. During that year, Marines endured tragic losses while attempting to restore peace in the war-torn country.

would provide the climate necessary for productive negotiations between the Israelis and Palestinians.

This was not the first time the Marines had been called on to assist in maintaining order in Lebanon. On 15 July 1958 US Marines landed south of Beirut and began to establish an armed perimeter around the city. Ordered by President Eisenhower at the request of then President Camille Chamoun, their mission was to protect the Chamoun government from a suspected *coup d'etat* by Communist forces. By the end of September some semblance of order had been restored and the Marines, praised for their restraint during the operation, left Beirut. The Mission causing them to return almost 25 years later was of a similar nature but this time the cost was tragic in its disproportion.

On 10 September 1982, the Marines returned to their ships offshore, having completed the task of evacuating Beirut. However, four days later the president of Lebanon, Bashir Gemayel, was assassinated and the Israeli Army moved back into Beirut to control the violence that seemed imminent. In a serious lapse of judgement the Israelis

allowed Christian Phalangists into Palestinian refugee camps; the resulting massacre of several hundred Palestinians by Phalangist extremists plunged the country into deeper turmoil. This prompted President Reagan on 29 September to authorize the Marines to again join the French and Italians in attempting to restore order. The Marines were given the task of guarding the Beirut International Airport, a task that was to become more difficult and costly than anyone could imagine.

One of the difficulties the Marines faced in guarding the airport resulted from being placed in a combat situation with the mission of keeping peace and not engaging in direct offensive combat. The Rules of Engagement (ROE) in Beirut were clearly spelled out and basically stated that Marines could fire back when fired upon but only when they could definitely determine that they were being *directly* fired upon and could absolutely identify a specific target. Even when these criteria were met word had to be passed up the chain of command and an answer passed back down before the Marines could return fire. Observers of this situation often described the Marines as sitting ducks.

***Both pages:* The aftermath of the terrorist attack on the US embassy in Beirut on 20 September 1984. Much of the building was demolished and two US servicemen were killed.**

Below: American and Lebanese rescue workers search the destroyed building that housed Marine Headquarters in Beirut. The headquarters was the target of terrorist attack on 23 October 1983 in which 241 Marines were killed.

Inset: The body of a Marine killed in Lebanon is loaded onto a C-130.

By 12 September 1983 there were 1200 Marines on shore and another 2000 on ships off the coast of Beirut. The Marines had begun to sustain casualties as a result of sniper fire, explosions and shelling. Though now authorized by the President to call in naval gunfire and air strikes if necessary to protect themselves, the essential nature of the mission remained the same and with it the same ROE. In the weeks that followed the Marines continued to exercise the restraint that they have often been praised for. This time, however, there was to be no reward and on 23 October a truck carrying 12,000 lb of explosives drove past the sentry guarding the compound where the Marines were headquartered and into the headquarters building. It was early in the morning and most of the men inside were still

Above: US Marines on patrol were a familiar sight for the citizens of Beirut in 1983.

Top and opposite top: Marine troops land at Landing Zone Red, and make an amphibious landing on Green Beach.

asleep. The resulting explosion killed 241 Marines, more than had died on any single combat action during the entire Vietnam War. Marine casualties in Beirut did not stop with the bombing. Questions about their role and presence there continued to be raised, resulting in a decision in early 1984 to withdraw all Marines from Beirut. It was a devastating time for the Marines, made worse because the nature of the mission had been so unclear and the cost so high. Still the Marines had been where they were asked to be, doing what they were asked to do, to the best of their ability.

A Marine patrols the ravaged streets of
Beirut. Amid the turmoil, the Marines
served with customary restraint until
their withdrawal in 1984.

Fortunately not all Marine operations have been as tragic and frustrating as Beirut. A good example is the Marines' involvement in Grenada. On 25 October 1983 some 400 Marines landed on Grenada. This time US intervention was no less controversial, but the mission was clear: to rescue nearly 1000 Americans, mostly students, at St George's University School of Medicine. It was feared that because of the turmoil caused when Prime Minister Maurice Bishop and about 100 other Grenadians were killed by a group of radical leftists, the Americans were in danger of becoming political hostages. The lessons learned from a similar situation in Iran prompted a direct approach to the problem.

Operation *Urgent Fury* began before daybreak when a four-man US Navy SEAL (sea, air and land) team parachuted to a position off the southern shore. Their mission was to provide battle commanders with intelligence concerning the Cuban-built 10,000-foot runway at Point Salines, but all four of them drowned in unexpectedly high seas. Because of the rough water, Battalion Landing Team 2/8 of the 22nd MAU were ferried ashore by helicopters from the US Navy helicopter carrier USS *Guam*. They proceeded to take Pearls Airport and secure the

Above: **A disabled Marine CH-46E, abandoned on Grand Anse beach on Grenada.**

Opposite top and bottom: **A Marine LVTP-7 amphibious vehicle, and Pearls Airport, used as a receiving point on Grenada.**

northern half of the island nation meeting with very little resistance. US Army Rangers, however, parachuting onto the southern half of the island near the Point Salines airport met with stiff resistance. Cuban workers living near the airstrip were more heavily armed than the Pentagon had expected and were using antiaircraft weapons against the Rangers. However, by 7:15 the Point Salines airport area had been cleared and US Air Force C-130s were able to land. Meanwhile, the *Guam* had moved around to the west coast sending 13 amphibious vehicles with 250 Marines and five tanks to take Fort Frederick and its Richmond Hill prison near Grenada's capital of St George's. As the Marines moved down from the north toward St. George's, the Army Rangers moved up from the south. Resistance from the Grenadian revolutionaries was again much heavier than expected and by nightfall of that first long day the military had still not secured the island. By early morning the next day most of the resistance had been put down and Marines stormed

252

the mansion where the British governor-general was beseiged. That evening Fort Frederick and the campus of the medical school were secured and by the morning of the 27th the Atlantic Fleet commander reported that all major military objectives had been secured. It was a brief operation, but not without casualties. Eighteen Americans were killed and 67 wounded. A week later all Marines had left the island and within six weeks only about 300 US Military Police and support troops were still on Grenada. There was a job to be done, the Marines were called in, and the operation was a success.

Memorial services for the heroes of both Lebanon and Grenada were held

Above: **Pearls airport was unofficially renamed MCAS Douglas, hence the sign.**

Below: **Documents and other items found in the soldiers' barracks on Grenada.**

at Cherry Point and Camp Lejeune on 4 November 1983. President Reagan spoke for the entire country when he said: 'America seeks no new territory, nor do we wish to dominate others. Yet we commit our resources and risk the lives of those in our armed forces to rescue others from bloodshed and turmoil, and to prevent humankind from drowning in a sea of tyranny. Today, the world looks to America for leadership. And America looks to its Corps of Marines....'

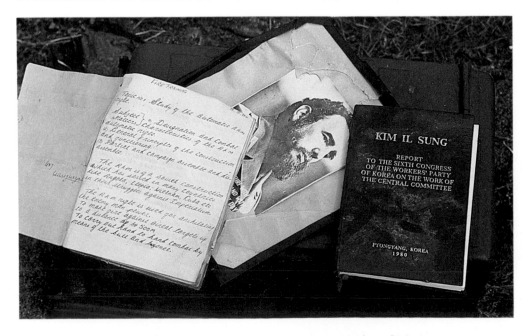

Above and left: Found on Grenada: ammo with North Korean markings, and a CH-53 about to lift a Russian antiaircraft gun.

Below: Two weeks after the headquarters bombing, Reagan discussed the tragic situation with Marines at Camp David.

AT WAR WITH TERRORISM

Operations like those in Beirut and Grenada have always been a part of the Marine Corps' mission but today Marines face a new and increasingly dangerous menace — international terrorism. In his address to Congress for fiscal year 1986, General Kelley made the Marines' role in combating terrorism a key topic, calling terrorism a new dimension in warfare that required the development of new and innovative techniques and strategies. Commandant Kelley described a seven-point program that the Marine Corps is adopting. The program is aimed at ensuring that every Marine is thoroughly aware of the terrorist threat, realistically trained and educated in how to counter the threat and armed with the best doctrine, tactics and equipment available. Efforts to provide field commanders with timely and accurate information regarding terrorist activity are being increased. Security is being tightened in order to deter terrorist attack against Marine Corps installations, facilities and deployed units.

The Marine Corps program to combat terrorism begins with coordination and monitoring of the program itself as it develops. This enables the Corps to provide centralized control at the Marine Headquarters level while establishing the agencies and working groups needed to effectively implement the measures that make up the program, monitor their success and evaluate possible improvements.

Secondly, the Marine Corps is constantly reviewing the terrorist threat and attempting to honestly assess its current capabilities to counter that threat. Since terrorism by its very nature is constantly changing, the Marines must remain capable of anticipating changes and quickly adjusting tactics, techniques, weapons and threat locations.

Intelligence, the third step, is provided by the newly established Terrorist Threat Section which interacts with other intelligence agencies addressing terrorism. This section attempts to identify specific threats to Marine Corps personnel or installations and provide timely information, recom-

Right: **Marines on maneuvers. War games are a part of a new antiterrorism program adopted by the Marine Corps. Troops are receiving extensive training to combat the threat of terrorism.**

mendations and intelligence assistance to the threatened command or region.

The fourth step being taken is to review and upgrade physical security. This includes the publication of a new security manual, acquiring new security equipment and dogs, enhancing military police training and preparing detailed security and crisis management plans.

Video tapes, films, war games, correspondence courses and mobile training teams provide some of the means to accomplish the fifth step of education. As General Kelley said during his address, 'An aware, alert, well-trained Marine is the key to defeating the terrorist.' In support of this education the

sixth part of the program provides publications on doctrine, tactics and techniques necessary for Marines and their commanders to fight the terrorist. Publications will range from policy and guidance for the commander to actual 'how to fight' techniques for the Marine on the ground facing the threat.

The final step is to enhance the ability of the Corps to operate in a terrorist environment by making certain organizational adjustments, particularly in the area of security and by establishing and publishing an operational standard to evaluate each unit's capabilities. As General Kelley told Congress, its purpose is 'to prove to enemies that terrorism is too costly a tactic to adopt against Marines.'

AMBASSADORS IN BLUE

The Marine Security Guards (MSG) are called America's Ambassadors in Blue. True to their motto, 'in every clime and place,' they are today serving in 127 detachments in 109 countries, protecting Americans abroad as Marines have been doing for over 200 years. However, they now have the added responsibility of being in the front line of the war against terrorism.

The MSG is an an elite group of nearly 1200 highly trained and lightly armed men whose job it is to guard American embassies, consulates, and legations around the world. Formally established by the Foreign Service Act

***Above and right:* MSG guards in their bullet-proof monitoring stations.**

of 1946, the guard is charged by the secretary of the Navy with providing enlisted men to meet the requirements of the Department of State for security guards at Foreign Service posts.

The MSG is a strictly volunteer outfit open to male Marines in the grade of lance corporal through master sergeant. Women Marines served briefly in this post during a test period in 1979–80. Though they aquitted themselves proudly, it was decided that the potential for incidents of terrorism or other hostile action was too high, making it a combat situation.

MSG volunteers are carefully

screened. They must be US citizens, and have the type of military and civilian record which will enable them to be granted a top-secret security clearance. The final requirement is that volunteers for the MSG below the rank of sergeant be unmarried. The unique situation of Post Security makes it a 24-hour mission requiring complete dedication and availability. In the event of an emergency it is felt that there would be insufficient time to secure the safety of dependents.

A Marine volunteer meeting these requirements reports to Marshall Hall, Quantico, VA for an initial training period of six weeks for sergeants and below. Senior Non-Commissioned Officers (SNCOs) train for eight weeks, the two additional weeks spent on administrative responsibilities normally assigned to an officer in any other Marine Corps assignment. After being assigned to a post, the SNCO will function as MSG commander, training NCO, administrative officer and foreign service liaison, and will be responsible to the senior American diplomat and accountable for the performance and

well-being of his detachment. This scope and latitude of responsibility is available to an SNCO only in the Marine Security Guard battalion.

MSG training is tough and much of the time is spent in a bullet-proof replica of Post #1, the access control point and monitoring station at every Marine Security Post. It is here that the Marine on guard must be able to detect even the slightest possibility of danger and remain cool and calm while responding to the situation presented. Meticulous care is given to uniforms. The trainee learns methods and procedures to ensure that his appearance is in keeping with the extremely high standards of the Guard.

Members of the Marine Security Guard battalion were in Iran to guard the embassy in 1979 and became part of what will be remembered in history as the Iranian Hostage Crisis.

Opposite: **An 'Ambassador in Blue.'**

Below and right: **The ill-fated Operation 'Evening Light' (rescue mission to Iran) gets underway. An RH-53 Sea Stallion lifts off and others prepare to follow.**

In February of 1979 Jimmy Carter began plans to send a contingent of 69 Marines and six helicopters to evacuate the 7800 Americans believed to be in Iran at the time. Before the plan could take effect however, the US embassy in Teheran was stormed. The 19-member Marine Security Guard tried to hold off the attackers by firing tear gas and later birdshot. These tactics were inadequate to deal with the magnitude of the attack and the Marines were forced to surrender. They were held with some 100 embassy employees, including Ambassador William Sullivan until representatives from the Ayatollah Khomeini arrived hours later and arranged their release. However, one Marine wounded in the attack and taken to a Teheran hospital was then kidnapped by supporters of Khomeini and held for a week before being released.

Iran continued to boil with internal unrest and to threaten the US with reprisals should any hospitality be granted Iran's deposed Shah. When President Carter finally allowed the Shah to enter the US for treatment of cancer on 22 October 1979, the pot began to boil over.

Sunday morning 4 November dawned with a mob outside the US embassy shouting 'Death to America,'

a scene the embassy personnel had become accustomed to. However, by 10:30 am demonstrators began to force the gate. The Marine guards acted with their usual restraint in holding off the mob. Their cool-headed response is credited with preventing the bloodshed it is felt would have been inevitable had they responded with fire. Thirteen Marines were among the 65 Americans taken hostage. Four black Marines and nine of the other hostages, five women and four other black men, were released two weeks later to show the terrorist's support for 'oppressed groups.' The remaining nine Marines, along with 41 other American men and two women were held in captivity for 444 days.

Since none of the appeals or negotiations to gain release of the hostages had been successful, on 11 April 1980 President Carter ordered a military rescue mission that had been in the planning stages since early in the crisis.

Marines were members of the combined-forces team that attempted the rescue and were given the task of piloting the eight RH-53D helicopters assigned to the mission. At least six of the aging helicopters were considered essential for success and when three failed with mechanical difficulties the mission was canceled. The remaining five began to refuel from the Air Force C-130s at the rendezvous site called Desert One. During this refueling procedure, one of the helicopters collided with a C-130 and the resulting fire and explosion of ammunition caused the other helicopters to burst into flame.

Top and above: **Sea Stallion helicopters and crewmen aboard the USS *Nimitz* in preparation for the aborted hostage rescue attempt on 11 April 1980, in which these aircraft were lost and three Marines were killed.**

Opposite: **A Marine in camouflage paint.**

Eight men were killed, among them three Marines. The wounded were carried aboard the C-130s but the intense fire prevented the retrieval of the dead and their bodies were left behind. In an unprecedented act of barbarism the Iranians put the charred bodies on display at the embassy compound before finally returning them to the United States. It was to be many more months before the hostages were finally released and this episode in America's nightmare in Iran closed.

Opposite: **The United States Marine Band, proud and splendid representatives of the Marine Corps spirit.**

Left: **Bandmaster and composer John Philip Sousa.**

THE PRESIDENT'S OWN

Almost as old as the Marine Corps itself, the United States Marine Band, started by Major William Burrows, was officially established by President John Adams on 11 July 1798. Marching the streets of Philadelphia to stir up recruits for the young Corps, the band had only a few poor instruments. Major Burrows was not to be discouraged and simply assessed each officer 10 dollars to pay for needed instruments. Today the band performs over 600 concerts annually and boasts 140 pieces.

The band made its White House debut on New Year's Day 1801 and shortly after moved into the Marine barracks at Eighth and I Streets in Washington, DC, where they remain housed to this day. The Marine Band is the oldest continuously active unit in the Marine Corps.

One of the more well-known instruments of the band in former years was the Marine Band Harmonica produced by Hohner and popular with John

Philip Sousa during his directorship of the Band from 1880 to 1892. The Marine Band Harmonica is still made by Hohner and is one of their more popular models, but today's more-symphonic USMC band no longer uses it in concert.

The Marine Band has played for every Presidential Inauguration since that of Thomas Jefferson, who is credited with giving the band the title 'The President's Own.'

Today's band has a number of performing ensembles, including the concert and marching bands as well as chamber orchestra, string ensembles, dance bands and a dixieland band, which tour at no expense to the taxpayer. Normally, sponsoring organizations charge an admission fee to help defray costs. Any profit made by a performance is donated to a local charity or civic project.

The United States Marine Band has seen no combat action in over 170 years. When they did it was in one of the more embarrassing actions in Marine history. Near the end of the War

Above: **The Marine Band Harmonica.**

Top two photos: **The Marine Band during two of their many annual performances.**

of 1812, members of the Marine Band joined a hastily assembled force that failed in an attempt to turn back the British, who then went on to sack the capital and burn the White House. Though the band did not go on to win fame in other battles, it has played during every war to boost the morale of the troops and civilians alike. During times of war or peace, the band continues to provide music not just for the president but for the entire country.

ARMED AND EQUIPPED TO FIGHT

Though emphasis in the USMC has always been on the quality of personnel, providing those men and women with the best materiel available is a high priority. Since the Marine mission is of an amphibious nature, one of the most important considerations is the transporting of troops and equipment from sea to land. The Marine Corps has come a long way from the row boats of 1775.

Today's state-of-the-art amphibious assault vehicle is the LCAC air-cushion landing craft which were first based at Camp Pendleton, California. The LCACs are designed primarily for amphibious assault and rapid movement of combat forces ashore, but their payload capacity of 60–75 tons and speed of 50 knots enhance the current heliborne assault capability by providing for early delivery of heavy weapons and equipment ashore. These new landing craft complement the AAVs (amphibious assault vehicles) already in use. The Marine Corps currently has 984 AAVs in use with another 327 on order. Plans for further modernization of the amphibious assault forces as well as service life extension programs (SLEPs) are expected to provide the Marine Corps with the

Opposite: **The improved semiautomatic M16A2 is the standard Marine rifle.**

Above: **The HAWK (Homing All the Way Killer) medium-range air defense missile.**

capability of simultaneous lift of both a MAB and a MAF by 1994.

Ground mobility is being increased by the delivery of a new one-and-one-quarter-ton cargo vehicle (CUCV) as well as a new five-ton tactical truck, of the M939 series, to replace existing 2.5 and five-ton vehicles. In addition plans are underway to replace existing trucks with a new one-and-one-quarter-ton high-mobility multipurpose wheeled vehicle (HMMWV), nicknamed 'Hummer,' within the next three years.

Ground firepower and combat mobility continue to be provided by the M60A1 Main Battle Tank with 550 currently in service. However, following successful testing, the new M1A1 was approved to begin replacing the aging M60s in fall of 1985.

The piece of equipment most essential to each Marine is still his rifle. The M16, designed in 1957 by Eugene M Stoner continues to serve the Marine Corps by providing either semiautomatic or fully automatic fire. The newly improved M16A2 version is semi- and three-round-burst automatic. It will replace the current inventory of fully automatic M16A1s by 1989.

A well-trained Marine and an up-to-date rifle are the initial building blocks

The Light Armored Vehicle (LAV) affords the Marines with a new flexibility in ground fire and maneuverability. The LAV was first fielded in 1984.

Opposite: **Landing vehicles, tracked personnel (LVTP), and Marines form a 'firing line' in front of two LVTP above.**

Above and right: **Two LCMs aboard the USS *Vancouver*, and M48 tanks at Camp Lejeune.**

of the Marine Corps, but it is the quick response and rapid deployment of thousands of Marines and tons of equipment and supplies that make the Marine Corps America's Force-in-Readiness. 1985 marked the beginning of a new program aimed at enhancing both.

The Maritime Pre-positioning Ships (MPS) concept will enable the Navy-Marine Corps team to provide a force of combined arms with 30 days of essential supplies already positioned at strategic points around the world. By the end of 1986, 13 specifically designed maritime pre-positioning ships carrying equipment and supplies sufficient for three 16,500-man brigades will be in position and ready to respond to any global crisis. Two MPS brigades were operational in 1985 and the third joined them in 1986. Construction of the cargo ships necessary to support the program has given a needed boost to the American shipbuilding industry.

The MPS program makes it possible

to respond to a crisis with full power in a fraction of the time it would take to transport both troops and equipment to a crisis area. Now, should the United States' interests be threatened anywhere in the world, an MPS squadron can alter course and arrive in a couple of days. Marines can then be airlifted to join their equipment and supplies on the MPS. The visibility of the MPS squadron can be controlled, allowing the US to project only the level of strength necessary to discourage a potential enemy while maintaining enough force nearby to meet with hos-

Above and above right: **A Marine aims an antiaircraft gun during maneuvers, and a maritime prepositioning ship (MPS) is loaded with essential supplies.**

tility should it become necessary. Each MPS squadron will take part in one Joint Chiefs of Staff-directed exercise per year.

Training exercises are the heart of the Marine Corps' ability to maintain a constant state of combat readiness. Exercises are held throughout the year and around the world. They include both Marines on active duty and Marine Reservists. It is at these mili-

Right and far right: **Marines arriving in Lebanon in May of 1983: MULES bring gear ashore (right) and Marines drive an M60 down the beach shortly after landing.**

tary exercises that Marines experience conditions from the frozen fjords of Norway to the sun-baked deserts of Egypt. Strategy and tactics are practiced and refined in a simulated combat atmosphere. In joint exercises with the Army, Navy and Air Force, Marines have the opportunity to practice the techniques necessary to function as part of a multiservice cohesive team.

Two AH-1T Cobra gunships reflect the dawn's early light. These attack helicopters have antiarmor capability.

Above and left: **Examples of Marine aircraft, including the CH-46F Sea Knight helicopter as it discharges troops, and the F/A-18 Hornet.**

MARINE CORPS AVIATION

From dive bombing in World War I to commanding the Space Shuttle in 1985, Marines have a proud aviation history spanning 73 years. Lt Alfred A Cunningham was assigned to the Navy's aviation camp at Annapolis, Maryland on 22 May 1912, becoming the first Marine to win his wings. By the time America entered World War I there were just 39 Marine Aviators. Because the Marines had no aircraft of their own in Europe, most of their

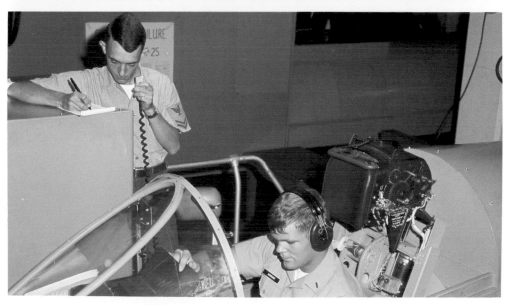

Above and right: **Flight simulators, such as these for the CH-46 helicopter and the A-6 attack plane, provide Marine aviators with invaluable training.**

flying was done with the British and French squadrons. By the end of World War I Marine Aviation had grown to nearly 2500 men.

Today there are about 4900 Marine Aviators. This is one of the careers not available to women in the Marine Corps because of the combat nature of the Marine air mission; however, women may be assigned to aviation support functions. Pilot training is available to all male commissioned officers who can meet the stringent requirements. It begins with 12 to 18

Above and left: **An EA6-B Prowler, used in electronic warfare, is serviced, and an MV-22A Osprey, which will eventually replace helicopters on many carriers.**

months at a Naval Air Training Command. The Navy trains Marine pilots and awards them Navy wings. The Navy also owns the aircraft that the Marines operate. Whether the pilots are called Naval Aviators or Marine Aviators is a subject of some debate, but there is no question that once wearing their wings and assigned to a squadron they are Marines.

The Navy has an annual budget of approximately 365 million dollars to train Navy, Marine Corps and Coast Guard pilots. All go through identical training until assignment to their individual service squadrons. The Marine Corps squadrons are jet fighters, jet attack, helicopter or multiengine transport. Marine Corps pilots fly some of the most up-to-date aircraft available and look forward to a twenty-first century that sees completion of programs now under development. One of the most exciting is the research and development of the MV-22A Osprey. This tilt-rotor aircraft will pro-

A Marine aviator poses with his F/A-18 Hornet. The Marine Corps uses the unusually versatile Hornet primarily as a fighter.

Above and left: The Sea Stallion CH-53D, and the CH-53E Super Stallion (left), which can lift all USN and USMC fighter, attack and electronic warfare aircraft.

vide the speed and efficiency necessary to replace the aging fleet of CH-46 helicopters by the mid-1990s. The MV-22A has been called the single greatest development in military aviation since the jet engine. Its 250-knot speed and lift capability coupled with its self-deployability and versatility far outstrip that of conventional helicopters, making it Marine Corps Aviation's highest-priority development program.

The CH-53E Super Stallion helicopter will complement the MV-22A by providing heavy-lift capability into the twenty-first century. The Super Stallion is rated at 16 tons of lift, making it capable of lifting 93 percent of all heavy equipment in a Marine Division, compared to 38 percent by its predecessor, the CH-53D Sea Stallion. In-flight refueling ability and two 650-gallon fuel tanks give the Super Stal-

Above and right: **The CH-46 Sea Knight, the principal assault helicopter for the Marine Corps. The interior is designed to accommodate personnel and supplies.**

lion an impressive range and combat capability.

In the air-to-ground and air-to-air role, the Marine Corps continues to rely on the F/A-18 Hornets. Reliable and remarkably easy to maintain, the F/A-18 completed 1984 with an 81 percent mission-capable rate and a heretofore unheard of 76 percent full-mission-capable rate. Man hours required to service the Hornet have been cut to less than half of those required to service its USMC predecessor, the F-4 Phantom.

The Marine Corps has also found the Harrier (V/STOL attack plane) to be an able complement to its fleet. The new McDonnell Douglas AV-8B Harrier II doubles the range and payload capabilities of the earlier British-built AV-8A. Funding is now being sought to upgrade the night-fighting capability of both the F/A-18 and the AV-8B,

Above and right: **The AV-8A Harrier two-seat trainer and the AV-8B Harrier. Both can take off and land vertically.**

Opposite, top: **The A-4M Skyhawk single-seat, light-attack bomber.**

as well as to provide two-seat trainer versions of the AV-8B.

The old A-6 Intruder continues to play an important role as an all-weather medium bomber. Plans to upgrade the current A-6E to A-6F include the introduction of new engines, improved radar systems and improvements aimed at increasing survivability and reliability.

Another aircraft in use in the Marine Corps since the 1950s is the A-4 Skyhawk, a single-engine, light-attack jet probably best known for its use by the US Navy's Blue Angels Squadron, a precision flying demonstration team traveling the world as 'Ambassadors of Goodwill.' Two Marine Corps pilots are currently members of this eight-man team. The Marine Corps provides transport for the Blue Angels in its own specially painted KC-130. The KC-130 is also used regularly for in-flight refueling and is affectionately called 'Fat Albert.'

One of the most important cargos transported by the Marine Aviators is the president of the United States. Sev-

eral VH-3D and VH-1N helicopters wear the title *Marine Corps One* with the designation HMX-1, and are used to carry the president from the White House lawn to a waiting US Air Force VC-137 jetliner designated *Air Force One. Marine Corps One* is also used for any short presidential junkets more appropriate to helicopter travel.

Marines have been in the air for 73 years and have now been traveling into space for 23 years. John Glenn, the first Marine in space and the first American to orbit the earth, flew the Mercury 6 mission on 20 February 1962 remaining in space for 4 hours 55 minutes and 23 seconds. Since then 12 Marines have been chosen for

NASA's astronaut program and 7 of them have already gone into space, including Colonel Robert F Overmeyer, the first Marine to command the Space Shuttle. Colonel Overmeyer was the pilot for STS-5, the first fully operational flight of the Shuttle Transportation System, which was launched from Kennedy Space Center on 11 November 1982, and commanded Space Shuttle Mission 51-B, launched on 29 April 1985. USMC Colonel Gerald P Carr is one of three astronauts holding the record for the longest time in space. Colonel Carr flew on Skylab 4 and was in space from 16 November 1973 to 8 February 1974. Colonel James F Buchli carried a bright red flag with

Top left and right: **The Blue Angels in formation, and the Marine C-130 that transports the team's equipment.**

Above: **Reagan boards *Marine Corps One*.**

Opposite: **Marine Col Robert Overmeyer commanding Space Shuttle mission 51-B.**

him when he boarded Shuttle Mission 51-C as Marine mission specialist on 23 January 1985. The flag, colors of the Commandant, was returned to General Kelley in a special ceremony. Colonel Buchli told the Commandant, 'Sir, the reason NASA picked a Marine for the mission was because we know the importance of the high ground, and you can't get any higher up than that.'

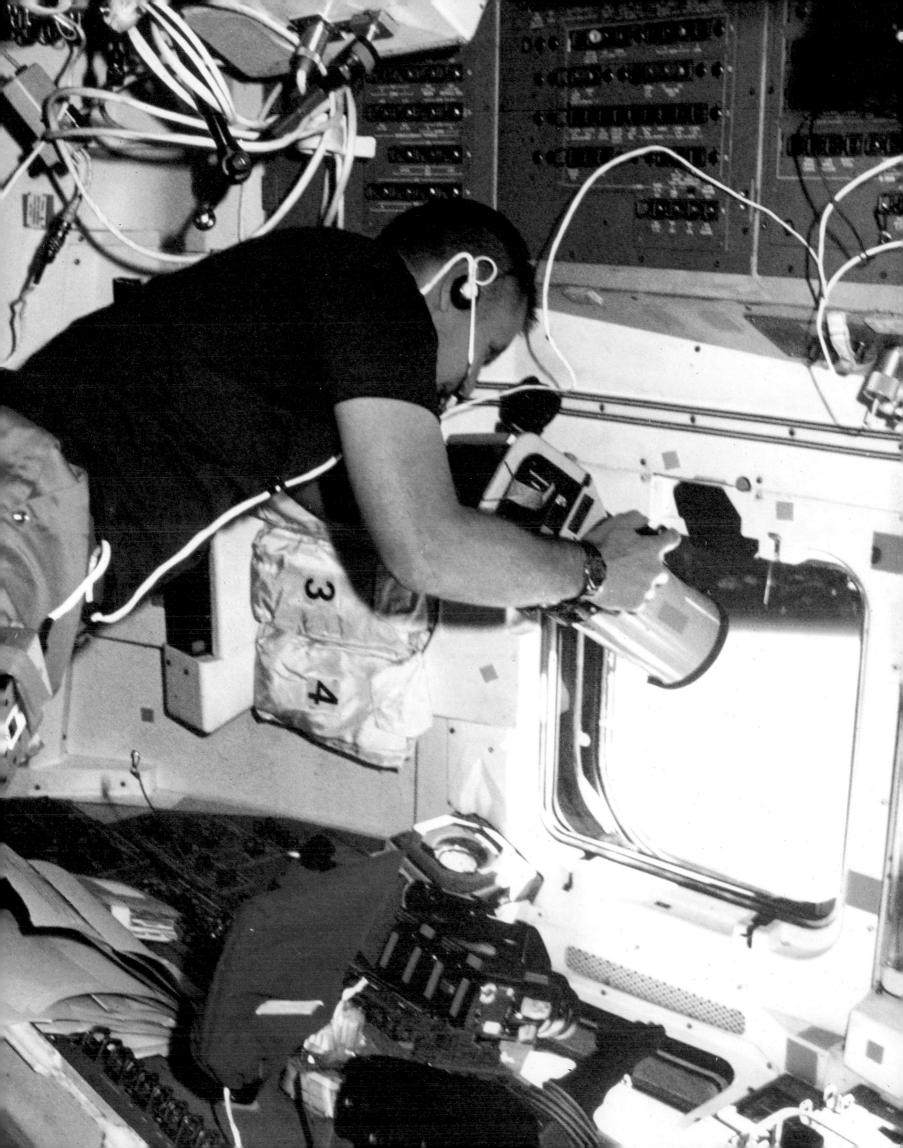

These A-4 Skyhawks are the same type of jets used by the Blue Angels, the Navy's precision flight demonstration team. Two Marines are currently Blue Angel pilots.

IN THE AIR, ON LAND AND SEA

Two hundred and ten years of pride and tradition stand behind the Marines of today. During those years the United States has always been able to rely on the Marines to go wherever they were sent and get the job done. In that service nearly 45,000 Marines have given their lives. Two hundred ninety-three Marines have earned the Medal of Honor, the nation's highest tribute. Of those, 120 lost their lives as a result of the action that earned them the medal.

What the future holds for the US Marine Corps and the nation it protects is impossible to guess. The threats we face today are certainly different from those we confronted dur-

ing the birth of our nation. Terrorism is becoming a major threat throughout the world, and because Marines have been chosen to protect our embassies and consulates abroad they are often directly in the line of fire in this most unpredictable of warfare. Recognizing this challenge, the Marine Corps is working hard to develop procedures and to train personnel to effectively fight and guard against the terrorist.

The United States remains dependent on the sea to protect our shores and to project our force around the world both as defense and as a deterrent to our enemies. The ability not only to deploy from both the sea and the air,

Opposite: **Marines in crisp dress blues.**

This page, left to right: **Marines in the field, deploying from a CH-46, and on amphibious assault maneuvers.**

Above: An F-4 Phantom ghosts across an eerie evening sky.

Left: **The Marine spirit of comradeship begins in boot camp and lasts forever.**

but to maneuver rapidly and effectively once on land are trademarks of the Marine Corps. The Maritime Pre-positioning Ships program is a tremendous advance in this direction making it possible for Marines and their equipment to reach any trouble spot in a matter of days.

There is no way of knowing when or where Marines will next be called into action — but their constant state of readiness, enhanced by recent operational and equipment advances and backed by more than 200 years of practice make them worthy of the nation's trust. The Marines, *Semper Fidelis.*

THE MARINE HYMN

From the Halls of Montezuma,
　　　　　To the shores of Tripoli;
We fight our country's battles
　　　　　In the air, on land, and sea;
First to fight for right and freedom
　　　　　and to keep our honor clean;
We are proud to claim the title of
　　　　　UNITED STATES MARINE.

Our flag's unfurled to every breeze
　　　　　From dawn to setting sun;
We have fought in every clime and place
　　　　　Where we could take a gun;
In the snow of far off northern lands
　　　　　And in sunny tropic scenes;
You will find us always on the job--
　　　　　THE UNITED STATES MARINES.

Here's health to you and to our Corps
　　　　　Which we are proud to serve;
In many a strife we've fought for life
　　　　　And never lost our nerve;
If the Army and the Navy
　　　　　Ever look on Heaven's scenes;
They will find the streets are guarded by
　　　　　UNITED STATES MARINES.

A Marine makes one last call to his sweetheart before shipping out on the USS *Cayuga* in the background.

THE UNITED STATES
AIR FORCE
TODAY

THE UNITED STATES
AIR FORCE
TODAY

BILL YENNE

Previous page: An Air Force Reserve F-16 fighter from Hill AFB, Utah, identifiable by its tail code and yellow marking on its vertical stabilizer.

Below: The B-1B will be America's major strategic bomber to the end of the century.

INTRODUCTION TO THE US AIR FORCE TODAY

The US Air Force is America's independent air arm, the organization charged with the air defense of the United States and her treaty allies whether North America under NORAD, or Europe under the NATO treaty.* Officially created on 18 September 1947, the US Air Force is nearly two centuries newer than the Army and Navy, but its lineage can actually be traced to the Balloon Corps Army of the Potomac (1861-63). The modern Air Force can be traced directly to 1 August 1907 when the Aeronautical Division of the US Army Signal Corps was created. From this arrangement evolved the US Army Air Service (USAAS) on 24 May 1918 — the height of World War I — which in turn became the US Army Air Corps (USAAC) on 2 July 1926.

On 20 June 1941, with World War II already raging in Europe and Pearl Harbor only 6 months away, the USAAC became the autonomous US Army Air Forces (USAAF) whose organi-

*The NORAD (North American Air Defense Command) treaty provides for joint United States and Canadian air defense of North America, while the NATO (North American Treaty Organization) treaty pools the resources of the United States, Canada and 16 Western European nations for the overall defense of Western Europe.

zation was to provide a blueprint for that of the US Air Force. During World War II the USAAF became the largest air force ever, with 2,373,292 personnel and 787,757 aircraft in 1944.

The US Air Force today is still the largest air force in the world in terms of personnel, with 597,125 men and women in uniform as of 1985. In terms of the number of aircraft, it ranks third, behind the Soviet Union and the Peoples Republic of China. However, while these two nations have enhanced their aircraft strength by retaining large numbers of planes built in the 1950s, half of the US Air Force inventory consists of aircraft built since 1970.

Of the roughly 7300 aircraft in the US Air Force inventory, 42 percent are tactical aircraft (interceptors, fighters, attack planes), 23 percent are trainers, 12 percent are transports, 8 percent are aerial refueling tankers, 5 percent are strategic bombers and 3 percent are helicopters. The remain-

Opposite: **Capt Jeff Kohler and his F-16 at Kunsan AB in Korea.**

Left: **Ground crewman Sgt Patricia Kiehne watches as her F-15 takes off.**

ing 7 percent range from reconnaissance and electronic warfare to utility and observation aircraft. These aircraft in the active US Air Force inventory are complemented by an additional 450 aircraft assigned to the Air National Guard (ANG). Of these 2050 additional aircraft 70 percent are tactical aircraft, 19 percent are transports, 7 percent are aerial refueling tankers; the rest include trainers, observation planes and helicopters.

Of the nearly 600,000 uniformed personnel in the US Air Force, 83 percent are enlisted airmen and 18 percent are officers. Nearly three-quarters of US Air Force personnel are sergeants and 15 percent are officers under the rank of lieutenant colonel. Practically a third of the total number of officers in the USAF are pilots and navigators, who number nearly 30,000.

Opposite: An F-16 Falcon, one of the USAF's top fighter-bombers, looms in the foreground at Beale AFB in California. Facing it is a C-5A Galaxy transport, one of over 60 that MAC operates.

Above: An Air Force security policeman, photographed by MSgt Ken Hammond, provides security for an Army air ambulance awaiting the arrival of the Beirut bombing victims at Ramstein AB.

Ten percent of the officers in the US Air Force are women and five percent are black. Of the enlisted personnel 12 percent are women and 17 percent are black. The average age of US Air Force personnel is 34 for officers and 26 for enlisted airmen. Sixty percent of the officers have college degrees while 39 percent have master's degrees and 2 percent have doctorates.

ORGANIZATION

The United States Air Force was established in 1947 by the National Defense Act of that year as one of the nation's three principal military forces contained within the Department of Defense. The Department of Defense (DoD) is headed by a civilian secretary of defense who has full cabinet rank on the president's cabinet. Under the secretary of defense are three civilian executive departments: Army, Navy and Air Force, each headed by a secretary who does not have full cabinet rank. Contained within each executive department are the small office of the secretary and a vastly larger military service.

The secretary of the Air Force is appointed by the president and like the other secretaries has an office at the Pentagon, a ten-minute drive from the White House and just across the Potomac River from Washington DC. The secretary's staff includes an under secretary, assistant secretaries for (a) manpower, reserve affairs and installations; (b) research, development and logistics and (c) financial management. Also on the staff are general counsel, the auditor general and whatever assortment of special assistants, administrative assistants and deputy under secretaries may be required at a given time. All of the above are civilian appointees, but the secretary may have US Air Force officers on his staff.

The US Air Force Air Staff is the military staff that commands the US Air Force and is headed by the chief of staff. Below the chief of staff are the vice chief of staff, the assistant vice chief and assistant chiefs for information, intelligence and studies and analysis. Also on the Air Staff are the judge advocate general, surgeon gen-

Air Force routine for some is folding the flag, chowtime, or catching a few winks on return from a deployment; but for others like Capt Appoloni and TSgt Baker *(opposite)* it's preparing to depart in their UH-1H Huey helicopter.

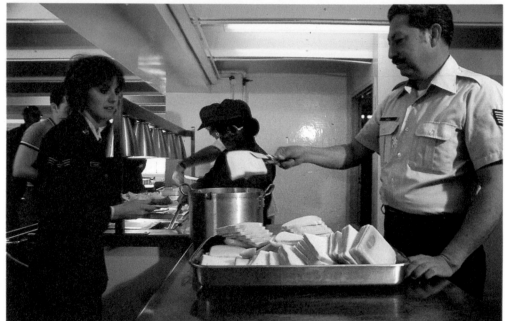

304

eral, chief of Air Force chaplains, director of administration, as well as the chief of the Air Force Reserve and director of the Air National Guard. All of the above are officers of general rank but the staff includes civilian scientists and one enlisted man, the chief master sergeant of the Air Force.

BASIC COMPONENTS

Within the Department of the Air Force and under the Air Staff there are three basic components to the full-time US Air Force — the Major Commands, the Direct Reporting Units (DRUs) and the Separate Operating Agencies (SOAs). The largest number of personnel (91 percent) are assigned to twelve Major Commands. Of the 750,000 total personnel in the Major Commands, 26 percent are civilians compared to 69 percent in the DRUs and SOAs.

In addition to the three full-time components of the US Air Force there are just over 200,000 reserve personnel in the Air National Guard (a DRU)

Above: **Chaplain Leslie G North at Charleston AFB. Airman Nancy Smelser photographed Capt North enthusiastically counseling a fellow worker.**

Below: **Airmen refuel an F-4 Phantom from a C-130 at a remote airfield. A UH-1 Huey helicopter overhead provides security for the operation.**

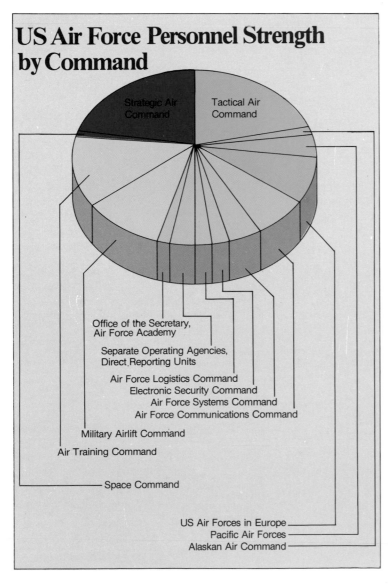

US Air Force Personnel Strength by Command

Strategic Air Command

Tactical Air Command

Office of the Secretary, Air Force Academy

Separate Operating Agencies, Direct Reporting Units

Air Force Logistics Command
Electronic Security Command
Air Force Systems Command
Air Force Communications Command

Military Airlift Command

Air Training Command

Space Command

US Air Forces in Europe
Pacific Air Forces
Alaskan Air Command

and the Air Force Reserve (an SOA) which would bring the total personnel strength of the US Air Force to slightly more than a million if they were all called up at the same time.

The Direct Reporting Units totaled 53,270 military and civilian personnel in 1985. The DRUs include the Air National Guard, the USAF Historical Research Center at Maxwell AFB in Alabama and the Air Force Technical Application Center (AFTAC), which has the responsibility within the Department of Defense to maintain the facilities and personnel to detect and monitor nuclear detonations in the atmosphere, underground and in outer space.

The Air Force Academy is also a Direct Reporting Unit. With the creation of an independent US Air Force in 1947, the need for a service academy, similar to those of the Army and Navy, became apparent. The US Air Force

Left: **Airman First Class Dana J Williams, photographed by TSgt Dennis Plummer performs maintenance on a portable power generator at Patrick AFB, Florida.**

Academy at Colorado Springs is discussed in greater detail beginning on page 92.

While each of the Major Commands and DRUs occupies a specific niche in the Air Force, each designed for a specific mission, the Separate Operating Agencies, totaling 26,288 military and civilian personnel in 1985, provide services to all the Commands, across the full breadth of the Air Force. The Air Force Accounting and Finance Center (AFAFC) based at Lowry AFB, Colorado is the centerpiece of a computerized global network of over a hundred accounting and finance offices (AFO) that issues paychecks, and conducts billings and collections. The Air Force Acquisition Logistics Center (AFALC) at Wright-Patterson AFB, Ohio works with the Air Force Logistics Command and the Air Force Systems Command to improve readiness and reduce costs in the systems acquired for use in the Air Force. The Air Force Audit Agency (AFAA), operating out of Norton AFB, California under the direction of the auditor general of the Air Force in the secretary's office, conducts evaluations of economy and effectiveness of Air Force operations. The Air Force Commissary Service (AFCOMS) operates from headquarters at Kelly AFB, Texas and fifteen sites in the US as well as two overseas regions (Europe and Pacific), managing 114 troop support operations worldwide. The purpose of AFCOMS is to purchase and provide food for all authorized Air Force appropriated-fund dining facilities.

The Air Force Engineering Services Center (AFESC) based at Tyndall AFB, Florida provides the Air Force world-

Above: **An Air Force sergeant checks a radar scope for malfunctions;** *(below),* **another sergeant works at her computer terminal. Security Police** *(opposite)* **guard Air Force resources with the help of dogs trained at Lackland AFB.**

wide with a broad range of important basic support services. These include readiness and contingency operations, facility energy, environmental planning, fire protection, installation operation and maintenance, food service, billiting and civil engineering.

The Air Force Office of Security Police (AFOSP) was established as an SOA in September 1979 at Kirtland AFB in New Mexico and placed under the command of the already existing office of Air Force chief of security police, who is answerable in both roles to the inspector general of the Air Force. The AFOSP operates the Air Force Security Clearance Office in Washington and is concerned with all

issues relating to the security of Air Force bases, personnel, systems and aircraft. While AFOSP has only about a hundred people, the worldwide Security Police Force that they support totaled 40,433 in 1985. In peacetime the Security Police Force (known as Air Police until 1967) functions much like a civilian police force. In wartime, with much tighter secrutiy imposed for possible enemy attack on USAF facilities, it would function more like an Army or Marine combat unit, with Air Base ground defense their primary mission. The tools of the security policeman's trade range from civilian-type police cars to armored vehicles, and from a wide variety of small arms to K-9 working dog teams. The last were used to aid the security arrangements at the 1984 Los Angeles Summer Olympics. AFOSP has also established a special antiterrorist branch to deal with the terrorist threat to USAF bases and facilities around the world.

The Air Force Office of Special Investigations (AFOSI), headquartered at Bolling AFB, District of Columbia, provides the Air Force and its commands with a broad range of investigative services including antiterrorist operations, counterintelligence, forensics, personnel protection and polygraph. More than half of AFOSI's activities deal with criminal investigations, and about a third deal with fraud in contracts, computer systems, property disposition, etc. The mission of the Air Force Inspection and Safety Center (AFISC) at Norton AFB, California is to assess USAF fighting capability and resource management and provide these assessments to the commands. The Air Force Intelligence Service (AFIS) based in Washington, DC gathers, evaluates and disburses intelligence information for Air Force Headquarters and USAF field commanders worldwide, as well as supplying intelligence for the Defense Department. The Air Force Legal Services Center (AFLSC), also in Washington, DC, is under the command of the judge advocate general. AFLSC functions as the Air Force's own inhouse law firm, handling claims for and against the Air Force, litigations, legal aid, labor law, etc. AFLSC provides legal services for the entire USAF ranging from patent and copyright protection to court-martial.

The Air Force Manpower and Personnel Center (AFMPC) is headquartered at Randolph AFB, Texas with its com-

308

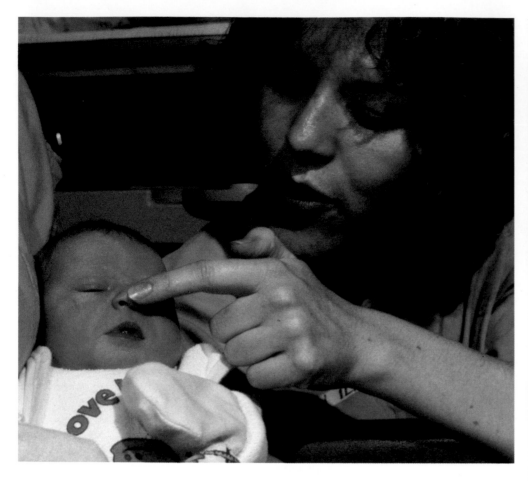

mander also serving as the assistant deputy chief of staff for manpower and personnel on the Air Staff. AFMPC administers the Air Force programs dealing with the lives and careers of USAF personnel and their families. The Air Force Office of Medical Support (AFOMS), headquartered at Brooks AFB, Texas was established in July 1978 as the Air Force Medical Service Center (AFMSC), becoming AFOMS in July 1985. AFOMS is under the command of the deputy surgeon general of the Air Force for operations. The AFOMS oversees health-care policy and practice within the Air Force as well as USAF medical research. There are two AFOMS directorates—Health Care Support and Professional Services, the latter located in the surgeon general's office in Washington, DC. The Air Force Operational Test and Evaluation Center (AFOTEC) at Kirtland AFB, New Mexico is charged with the testing of Air Force procedures, systems, and hardware under operational conditions. The Test and Evaluation Center has detachments based at Edwards AFB, California; Eglin AFB, Florida; Nellis AFB, Nevada; and Kapuan AS in Germany.

The Air Force Service Information and News Center (AFSINC) headquartered at Kelly AFB, Texas is the in-house communications department

Air Force medic Lt Jan Cookson *(above)*, tickling the nose of a newborn at Yokota AB, Japan, and *(opposite)* A1C Vicki LeBlanc, anticipating her duties as an operating room technician during a simulated *Reforger* operation in Germany.

for the Air Force, providing information for Air Force as well as Army personnel through both print and broadcast media. AFSINC was founded in June 1978 and merged with the Air Force Hometown News Center one year later. The Army Hometown News Center became part of AFSINC in October 1980. AFSINC is composed of five directorates: the Air Force Office of Youth Relations, which provides liaison between the Air Force and such organizations as the Boy Scouts and the Girl Scouts; Administration & Resources; Internal Information; Armed Forces Radio & TV; and the Army & Air Force Hometown News Service. The Radio and TV Directorate manages all Air Force broadcasting throughout the Pacific, in Alaska, Europe, Greenland and the Middle East. The Air Reserve Personnel Center (ARPC) headquarters in Denver, Colorado is charged with maintaining the staff and reserves to administer the call-up of Air Reserve forces in time of national emergency. Its files contain data on 100,000 Air National Guard, 70,000 Air Force Reserve and 80,000 former active-duty personnel.

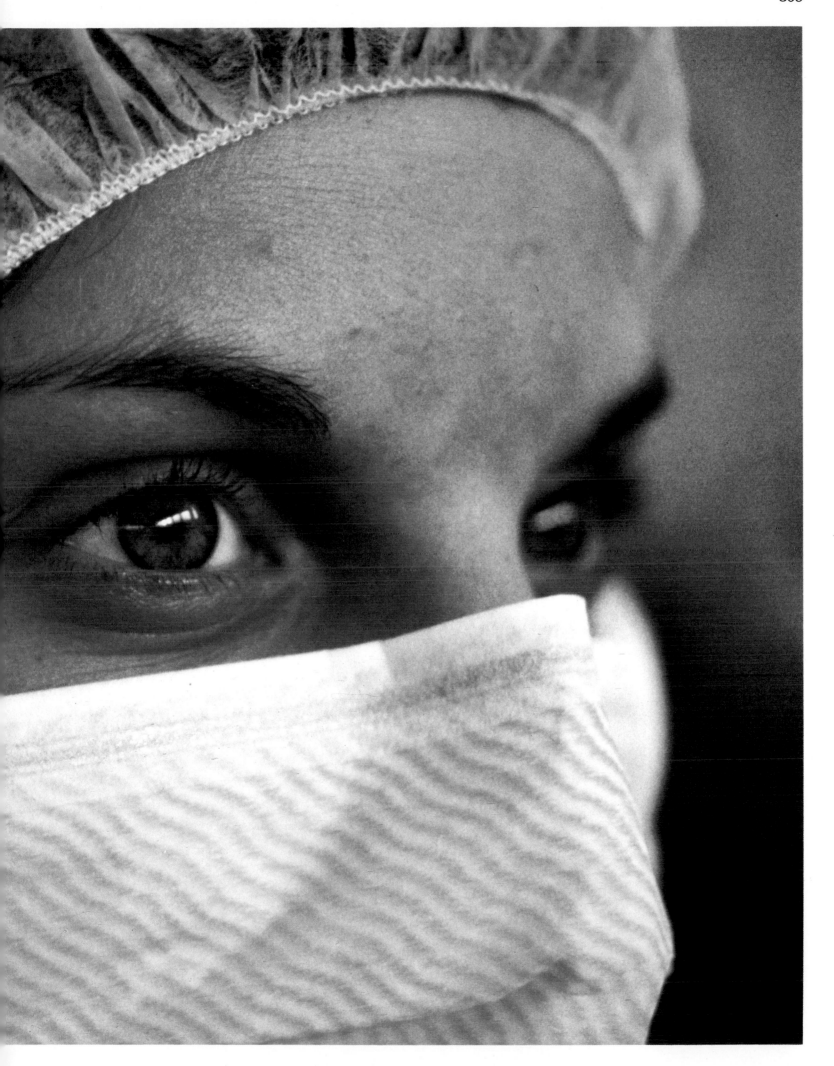

THE US AIR FORCE MAJOR COMMANDS

TACTICAL AIRPOWER

While the Direct Reporting Units and Separate Operating Agencies account for a large number of organizations, nine out of ten Air Force personnel are found in the Major Commands, with three out of those nine assigned to the four tactical commands: The Tactical Air Command (TAC), the Alaskan Air Command (AAC), the Pacific Air Forces (PACAF) and the United States Air Forces in Europe (USAFE).

Tactical airpower by definition involves the use of combat airpower in warfare, either defensively or offensively, toward an immediate tactical goal. Tactical airpower includes support of land or sea forces in battle, interception of enemy aircraft attacking one's homeland or one's forces behind the lines, interdiction of enemy forces and supply routes behind *his* lines and achieving air superiority over a battlefield or theater. Tactical airpower also includes tactical reconnaissance, which can be defined as the gathering of intelligence (from the air) to support tactical land, sea or air combat operations.

Opposite: **A TAC F-15 Eagle screams into the stratosphere.**

Above: **An F-15 pilot checks a Sidewinder AAM (blue indicates an unarmed practice missile).**

If tactical airpower is the basic building block of an air force, the fighter aircraft is the basic building block of tactical air power. Fighters, generally known until World War II as pursuit planes, are relatively small, fast and highly maneuverable when compared to bombers, the other major type of combat aircraft. The primary mission of the fighter is to fight other aircraft, whether dueling with other fighters for air superiority or intercepting enemy bombers. The interceptor is a fighter designed primarily to attack intruding enemy aircraft. The secondary mission of the fighter is to attack, with bombs, rockets or guns, enemy ground positions in the tactical ground-support role. Fighters engaged in this type of mission are called fighter-bombers and are distinguished from the other principal tactical aircraft (light bombers or attack planes, including such sub-types as dive bombers and torpedo bombers) by the fact that they could convert themselves to fighters at any time by jettisoning their bombs.

Attack aircraft or light bombers are two aircraft usually in the same size and weight class as fighters, but they

most often trade the speed and maneuverability required of a fighter in air-to-air combat for the ability to carry a heavier load of air-to-ground ordnance.

As of 1985, there were 3328 tactical aircraft in the US Air Force inventory, 531 'A'-designated attack planes and 2797 'F'-designated fighters. There were 464 of the new Fairchild Republic A-10 Thunderbolts with an average age of 4 years. Known informally by its crews as the 'Warthog,' the A-10 is a heavily armed and armored aircraft designed as a tank-buster. The balance of the attack fleet was divided between 23 Vought A-7 Corsairs and 44 Cessna A-37 Dragonflys. With average ages of 14 and 12 years respectively, these aircraft types had both

Above: **During TAC exercise *Leading Edge II*, TSgt Boyd Belcher photographed Lt Col Ron Daskevich looking confident in his uploaded F-16 at Nellis AFB, Nevada. The 388th TFW of Hill AFB was deployed to Nellis for the exercise.**

seen service at the end of the Vietnam War.

On the fighter side, the USAF inventory is divided between the Century series fighters left over from the 1950s, fighter types introduced in the 1960s during the Vietnam War, and the latest types introduced in the late 1970s and early 1980s. Of the Century series, there were 12 North American F-100 Super Sabres with an average age of 27 years and 64 Convair F-106 Delta Daggers with an average age of 25

years, the latter being gradually replaced as front-line interceptors by the F-15. Of the Vietnam-era types, in 1985 there were 339 General Dynamics F-111 Aardvarks with an average age of 13 years, 101 Northrop F-5 Tigers with an average age of 9 years, and 842 McDonnell Douglas F-4 Phantoms with an average age of 15 years. There were more Phantoms in the US Air Force than any other type of aircraft. Of the newest aircraft types there were 697 McDonnell Douglas F-15 Eagles with an average age of 5 years and 671 General Dynamics F-16 Falcons with an average age of just 2 years in 1985. Both of these planes, which represented the very best the American aircraft industry had to

Above: **All part of TAC: an F-16 in flight over the Panama Canal Zone** *(top),* **Lt Matt Dorschel and Lt Joe Paulette reviewing forms prior to takeoff in their F-4** *(left),* **and SSgt Guster Jones checking the battery compartment of an OA-37B Dragonfly** *(right).*

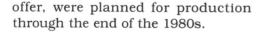

offer, were planned for production through the end of the 1980s.

TACTICAL AIR COMMAND

Tactical airpower has been an important part of the US Air Force and its predecessors since the First World War. Today the Tactical Air Command (TAC) and the Strategic Air Command (SAC), the US Air Force's two largest Major Commands, are roughly equal in personnel strength. In 1985 they had uniformed personnel strengths of 102,912 and 105,979 (114,402 and 118,064 including civilians) respectively. While SAC is the only strategic air command, TAC has more aircraft, and is the centerpiece

of the USAF's tactical airpower, which also includes three major regional, or theater, commands with additional personnel and aircraft: the Alaskan Air Command (AAC), the Pacific Air Forces (PACAF) and the United States Air Forces in Europe (USAFE).

TAC is responsible for training the pilots and developing the weapons and tactics which are rotated into the front-line regional commands. It is a measure of TAC's importance that in the late 1970s two Major Commands with a tactical mission were integrated into TAC. The United States Air Forces Southern Command (USAFSO), headquartered at Albrook AFB in the Panama Canal Zone, became the USAF Southern Air Division under TAC control, and the division headquarters were relocated to Howard AFB in the Canal Zone. In June 1979, the Aerospace Defense Command (ADCOM or ADC), responsible for the Nation's air defense and the major American component in the joint US-Canadian North American Air Defense Com-

mand (NORAD), became part of TAC; its commander became TAC deputy commander for air defense.

The Tactical Air Command and the Aerospace Defense Command (known as the Air Defense Command until 1 January 1968), the core of today's TAC, were both founded as Major Commands on 21 March 1946 along with the Strategic Air Command. These three Major Commands were designed to incorporate the heart of USAAF combat airpower and become the basic structure of the new USAF which would come into being 18 months later.

The mission of the Tactical Air Command is to organize, train, equip and maintain a highly mobile tactical air force capable of deployment anywhere in the world either on its own, through one of the three major regional commands (as it did through PACAF in Southeast Asia), or through the Rapid Deployment Force (RDF). The mission includes all the classic elements of tactical airpower: air superiority, air interdiction and close air support as well as tactical air reconnaissance, tactical electronic combat (electronic countermeasures, jamming, etc) and tactical air control (control of tactical combat aircraft). TAC is the US Air Force's mobile strike force — able to deploy

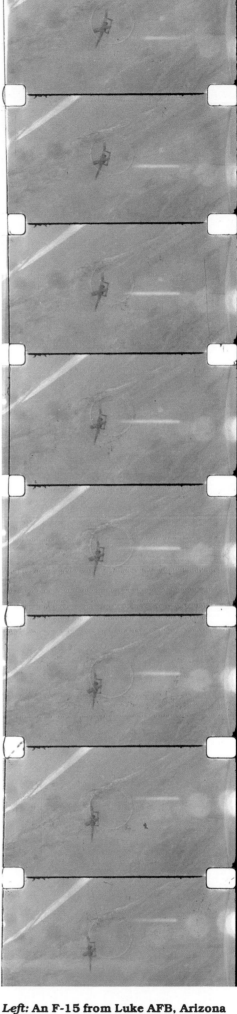

Left: An F-15 from Luke AFB, Arizona flies low over the Grand Canyon.

Above: An A-10 Warthog caught in the gunsights and gun cameras of an F-5 during *Red Flag* exercises over Nevada.

US general purpose air forces anywhere in the world on a moment's notice for tactical air operations in support of national security, and to provide combat-ready forces to defend North America against aerospace attack.

As part of its mission, TAC is each year involved in dozens of realistic tactical air exercises in the United States (such as the annual joint US-Canada air defense exercise code-named *William Tell*), Canada, Egypt (*Bright Star*), Germany, Italy and Korea. One of the most important parts of TAC training is a series of exercises designed by General Robert Dixon (TAC Commander 1973-78). These exercises, known as 'Flags,' were developed in the late 1970s to give USAF personnel practical, highly realistic training to prevent repetition of the mistakes that had plagued Air Force operations during the war in Southeast Asia.

Red Flag, the best known of the *Flag* exercises, takes place several times a year for six-week periods at the huge Air Force Bombing and Gunnery Range north of Nellis AFB in the tip of Nevada. The objective of *Red Flag* is to provide fighter pilots with realistic air-to-air combat missions.

To get combat experience, you have to go into combat against the enemy, so TAC created an 'enemy.' The TAC 4440th Tactical Fighter Training Group was formed at Nellis AFB. It is against the 4440th that pilots flying in *Red Flag* do mock battle.

Opposing aircraft are shot down by computers rather than guns, but in every other respect *Red Flag* is like the real thing, with the Aggressors flying with Soviet tactics as well as markings.

Blue Flag trains Command Control and Communications (C^3) personnel to ply their vital trade under wartime conditions. Training is tailored to simulate theaters in which the C^3 crews might have to operate, such as Europe, Korea or the Persian Gulf.

Checkered Flag is the exercise under which TAC units from stateside deploy to overseas bases from which they would have to operate in an emergency. The crews learn the peculiarities of a given base, the runway, the local weather, the facilities available, etc.

Copper Flag, is the Air Defense TAC (ADTAC) equivalent to *Red Flag* in which air defense crews, both air and ground-based, practice defending

Both pages: **More scenes from TAC include** *(opposite)* **an ECM pod being loaded on an F-16 during** *Leading Edge II, (above)* **Capt Jack Wooster conducting a night operations class,** *(right and below)* **1st Lt Susan Fiedler watching her aircraft tracking scope, TSgt Charles D Richard Heckerman checking the pack on an F-15 during** *Border Star 85,* **and** *(top)* **not an exercise — F-15 Eagles intercept a Soviet Tu-95 off the coast of the US.**

Right: AAC air traffic controllers keep a watchful eye on their radar screens during *Brim Frost 83.*

Below: These two F-16 Falcons were captured on a dawn patrol by aviation photographer George Hall as they streaked through the sky.

against enemy tactical air or strategic air attack.

Green Flag trains tactical air forces in the use of Electronic Warfare (EW) and Electronic Countermeasures (ECM). It is the electronic warfare counterpart of the other *Flags.* Once a year one of the *Green Flag* exercises is held at Nellis AFB in coordination with a *Red Flag* exercise.

ALASKAN AIR COMMAND

Just below the Arctic Circle in the Bering Strait, there is a place where one can stand in the United States and look at the territory of the Soviet Union only two miles away. The place is on the Little Diomede Island, Alaska, where only a thin strip of water (in winter, passable ice) separates the world's two superpowers. This proximity of Alaska to the Soviet Union underscores the importance of the Alaskan Air Command to overall security of the United States. The cold and loneliness make Alaska's remote corners a cruel and forbidding place, but also a place of stark and awesome beauty. As the prophet of air power himself, Billy Mitchell, said in 1935, 'Alaska is the most strategic place in the the world.'

The Alaskan Air Command (AAC) was created on 18 December 1945 by redesignation of the World War II-era Eleventh Air Force. The AAC headquarters was moved from Adak Island to Elmendorf Field (Elmendorf AFB since 1947) near Anchorage on 1 October 1946 where it has remained since. With the onset of the Cold War, the primary mission of the AAC was to provide early warning of possible Russian air attack coming over the polar route and to shoot down Russian bombers. With the mission of flying combat air patrol over the roof of the North American continent, AAC has taken the motto 'Top Cover for America.' The AAC interceptor units were initially equipped with P-51s

SSgt Thomas Groat *(right)* processes Capt Carl Bradshaw through customs after his flight from Eilson AFB, Alaska to Suwon AB, Korea for *Team Spirit 84.* Photo by MSgt Ken Hammond.

which were replaced in succession by F-80s, F-94s, F-89s, F-102s, F-4s and, in 1983, by F-15s. The peak aircraft strength (200) for the AAC was reached in 1957 (when F-89s were the first-line interceptor) and has declined ever since. In 1985 there were 7580 uniformed and 1178 civilian personnel assigned to AAC.

The Alaskan Air Command is also responsible for a radar network across the state designed to provide early warning of a possible Soviet air attack. The original 12-site network was constructed between 1950 and 1958. In 1973 the *Saber Yukon* study showed that the system was in need of upgrading and the *Seek Igloo* program was undertaken. Under *Seek Igloo,* an 11-site network of General Electric AN/FPS-117 remotely operated radar sites was built in Alaska between 1979 and 1984.

PACIFIC AIR FORCES

The Pacific Air Forces (PACAF), the air component of the US Pacific Command, were originally called the Far East Air Forces (FEAF). The FEAF had been created during World War II by a merger of the Fifth and Thirteenth Air Forces; the Seventh Air Force was added later in the war. On 1 July 1957 FEAF officially became the Pacific Air Forces (PACAF), the single USAF command for the Pacific Theater, with two numbered Air Forces — the Fifth in Japan and the Thirteenth in the Philippines. Both of the other numbered Air Forces, the Seventh in Hawaii and the Twentieth on Okinawa, had been dissolved since 1955. The command headquarters was moved to Hickam AFB adjacent to the US Navy's base at Pearl Harbor, Hawaii. PACAF began with 89,679 per-

Opposite: F-4s line up at the hot check area of Osan AB during *Team Spirit 84.*

Below: An F-16 is quick turned at Kunsan AB, Korea during *Team Spirit 84.*

Opposite and above: During exercise *Opportune Journey 4,* Sgt Judy Busselman, 3d AGS crew chief, is informed of and checks an F-4 cockpit malfunction.

Left: Maintenance is done on an F-15 during *Team Spirit 84.*

sonnel and 959 aircraft (including 152 F-100s and 249 F-86s), but by the time PACAF was called to take part in sustained operations in Southeast Asia in 1964, personnel strength had been reduced to 65,155 with 582 aircraft (including 110 F-102s and 153 F-105s) in the inventory.

With the rapid escalation of the war in Southeast Asia and PACAF's having been given the prime responsibility for USAF air operation, command strength rose rapidly to a peak of nearly 170,000 personnel and 2100 aircraft prior to the bombing halt in 1968. The Seventh Air Force was reactivated at Tan Son Nhut AB in South Vietnam and PACAF found itself operating from 18 bases in Southeast Asia,

A *Team Spirit 85* scrapbook: 563d TFS crews are greeted by Korean girls at Suwon AB *(above)*; PACAF airmen build a tent city *(top)*, personnel from Osan AB are evaluated during a simulated chemical attack *(left)*; USAF and Korean crews share communications chores *(below)*; while members of the 44th TFS *(right)* exercise their chemical warfare training. Cooperation and efficiency operated fully throughout *Team Spirit 85*.

Right: TSgt Lou Hernandez photographed Airman Pearce moving a bomb into place.

Both pages: Scenes from PACAF's *Team Spirit 85*, Osan AB, Republic of Korea.

Above: A pensive moment during a lecture on personnel management by Capt Chuck Courtney from PACAF Headquarters.

Left: A SWAT team apprehends a member of the 'opposing force' that jammed the airways during exercise *Commando Shoe.*

Below: This rapid runway repair exercise was photographed by SSgt Steve McGill.

including ten in South Vietnam, seven in Thailand and Ching Chuan Kang (Republic of China) AB on Taiwan. As more and more of the responsibility for the conduct of the air war was turned over to the South Vietnamese and tactical aircraft assigned to PACAF were gradually returned to TAC and reserve units, PACAF returned to its prewar strength. By 1975 the Seventh Air Force had ceased to exist.

In 1985 PACAF had a personnel strength of 36,612 (including 9171 civilians), with qualitative improvements in aircraft strength in the form of F-15 aircraft now assigned to the 313th Air Division on Okinawa and in Japan and F-16s to the 314th Air Division in Korea. While its numbers have stabilized, PACAF's responsibility, as that of the US Pacific Command, has increased. Once primarily responsible for the Pacific, the Pacific Command and PACAF now have responsibility for the Indian Ocean region as well, an

Scenes from the Pacific Air Forces at work: A 'cavalryman' fresh from a perimeter patrol at Clark AB in the Philippines *(top left)*; pilots from the 3d TFW walk to their F-4Es *(center)*; airmen cook their chicken in a fire pit during survival day training, held in the Crow Valley Range, near Clark AB. SSgt Fred Allison adjusts the fastener on a pylon that holds an Mk82 bomb *(far left)*; MSgt Michael Steinbeck whistles to his men *(left)*, but will they recognize him in camouflage paint? Combat control team member David Hawn *(above)*, handles a 'reptile assault' during an exercise near Sunchany, Korea.

Below: A panorama of the ramp area at Clark AB in the Philippines. In the foreground is a shark-faced F-4 Phantom of PACAF's 3d Tactical Fighter Wing. The 3d TFW is a major component of PACAF's 13th Air Force, which was created during World War II and has been based at Clark AB since the end of the war. Clark AB has a long and colorful history dating back to before World War II when it was Clark Army Air Field. In December 1941, Clark-based P-40 s (the forerunners of this Phantom) held off the Japanese invasion of the Philippines for the better part of a month against overwhelming odds. Behind the Phantom are a pair of KC-135 Stratotankers,

part of the aerial refueling contingent of the Strategic Air Command's Third Air Division headquartered on Guam. These tankers help provide aerial refueling support for US Air Force activities throughout the Pacific area.

Right: Another shark-faced F-4 Phantom from PACAF's 13th Air Force waiting to be loaded with a pallet of bombs *(foreground)* prior to taking part in a training mission during *Team Spirit 84.* The *Team Spirit* exercises are held annually in the Republic of Korea and draw on units from throughout PACAF as well as other Major Commands in the US Air Force.

area that stretches from the east coast of Africa to the west coast of the Americas, an area of more than a hundred million square miles or half the surface of the earth.

US AIR FORCES IN EUROPE

Since the end of World War II Europe has been generally acknowledged as the most likely place for a major-power confrontation that could lead to World War III. To meet this threat, the United States Air Forces in Europe (USAFE) were organized as a Major Command of the new USAF in 1947. USAFE was formed out of the tactical air assets left in Europe after the postwar demobilization and is today the second largest (after TAC) tactical command in the Air Force. Its 1985 personnel strength was 71,477 (including 9977 civilians). USAFE operates nearly 800 tactical aircraft and has over 1500 preassigned TAC aircraft in the United States that could be in place in Europe within 30 days. The aircraft are assigned to bases on both continents through the Co-located Operating Base (COB) program. USAFE is the largest of the regional commands, with over 60,000 uniformed personnel. Headquartered at Ramstein AB in Germany, it is the American contribution to the Allied Air Forces Central Europe (AAFCE), the tactical air component of the North Atlantic Treaty Organization (NATO). USAFE is composed of three numbered Air Forces: the Third, Sixteenth and Seventeenth.

The USAFE Seventeenth Air Force, based at Sembach AB along with the Luftwaffe of the German Federal Republic (Bundesrepublik Deutschland, BRD), is the major air element in NATO defense of Central Europe. The area is among the most critical because it faces the largest concentrations of Soviet and Warsaw Pact land and air power. All of the bases of the Seventeenth are located in the BRD with the exception of the 32d Tactical Fighter Squadron (TFS) based at Camp New Amsterdam near Soesterberg in the Netherlands. Flying F-15s, the 32d TFS is under joint operational control of the Seventeenth Air Force and the Netherlands Air Defense Center, as its primary role is to work with the Royal Netherlands Air Force (Koninklijk Luchtmacht Nederland, KLN) to maintain allied air superiority over the Netherlands in the event of

Above: **This USAFE F-4G 'Wild Weasel' from Ramstein AB is airborne over Germany. Note the several antiradar missiles attached to the aircraft.**

Below and right: **Sgt Ramsey buttons a turboprop engine intake at Aviano AB, Italy, while TSgt Wimbrow of the Security Police checks a perimeter line.**

war. There are six fighter wings assigned to the Seventeenth Air Force, all headquartered in the BRD, and flying A-10s, F-4s, F-15s, F-16s and RF-4s. Also in Germany, historic Tempelhof Central Airport in Berlin is maintained as an American support base, and the Military Airlift Command (MAC) has its 435th Tactical Airlift Wing based at Rhein-Main AB across the runway from Frankfurt's Rhein-Main Airport, Germany's major international air hub. Rhein-Main AB is also the major MAC air cargo hub for supplies being delivered to American forces in Germany, but much of the traffic is now going into Ramstein AB because of the growing civilian operations at Rhein-Main Airport.

The Third Air Force, headquartered at RAF Mildenhall in England, is USAFE's largest in terms of personnel and facilities. While the Seventeenth has the bulk of USAFE's tactical combat aircraft, the Third provides support facilities through nine RAF bases in southern England. In addition to supporting rotational MAC airlift operations and SAC strategic reconnaissance and air refueling operations, the Third has two tactical fighter wings flying F-111 fighter-bombers, one with A-10 attack aircraft and a tactical recon wing with RF-4s. The latter has an 'Agressor' Squadron, the 527th TFS flying F-5s in *Red Flag*-type exercises. The Third Air Force also has a civil engineer and heavy repair squadron at RAF Wethersfield and its 501st

Below: Two F-15 Eagle fighters from the 36th TFW of Bitburg AB, Germany.

Opposite, bottom: A maintenance crew at Aviano AB, Italy hooking a crane to a new engine during mobility testing.

Tactical Missile Wing at RAF Greenham Common, while the 485th Tactical Missile Wing at Florennes, Belgium support the deployment of the BGM-109G Ground-Launched Cruise Missile (GLCM).

USAFE units across southern Europe and into Asia Minor are under the command of the Sixteenth Air Force headquartered at Torrejon AB in Spain. The Sixteenth has a Tactical Fighter Training Wing (the 406th) at Zaragoza AB, Spain and a Tactical Fighter Wing (the 401st) flying F-16s at its home base of Torrejon. In addition there are three bases in Italy: San Vito AS, a support and communications station; Comiso AS, where the 487th Tactical Missile Wing supports the Ground-Launched Cruise Missile; and Aviano AB in northern Italy, a major support and refueling base. Aviano AB's refueling function is important for USAFE and other NATO aircraft because combat aircraft are not permitted to routinely overfly neutral

Above: **During NATO exercise *Cold Fire*, Sgt Dean Hensley receives a report of the opposing fire team's location.**

Opposite: **The pilot of an F-16 Fighting Falcon squints into the two o'clock sun while in flight over Europe.**

Austria and Switzerland and routing them over France eats a lot more fuel than a direct Germany-to-Italy flight. Bases in Greece and Turkey support both USAFE tactical operations and electronic surveillance of military activities in the southwestern part of the Soviet Union and the southern flank of the Warsaw Pact.

USAFE's mission today is to work with other NATO air forces to provide for the air defense of Western Europe and to support NATO ground forces defending Western Europe in the event of a Soviet and/or Warsaw Pact invasion. USAFE also monitors Soviet and Warsaw Pact activities during peace time and provides support for MAC and SAC units operating in Europe.

In 1977 USAFE was the first regional Major Command to receive the F-15 Eagle air-superiority fighter and the A-10 'Warthog' tactical air-support attack aircraft, both the top aircraft of their respective types. In 1980, the first of the G model of the F-4 Phantom, the 'Wild Weasel' or surface-to-air missile (SAM) suppressor version, made its appearance with USAFE units. Two years later, the F-16 fighting Falcon, a fighter/fighter-bomber with the advanced capabilities of the F-15, made its debut with USAFE.

USAFE participates with other NATO forces as well as US Army units in a number of training exercises such as *Reforger* and *Crested Cap* from Norway to the Mediterranean every year. USAFE is, of course, also a participant in the *Flag* exercises. In recent years these exercises have included training personnel to perform ground operations in chemical warfare protection suits and the development of procedures for rapid runway repair.

STRATEGIC AIR COMMAND

The Strategic Air Command (SAC) was created at the same time as the Tactical Air Command and the Air Defense Command (21 March 1946). It is the US Air Force's long-range strike force, deterring nuclear war by being ready to fight a nuclear war. In addition, it supports other operations by maintaining heavy bombers for conventional bombing missions and aerial refueling tankers to serve the entire US Air Force. SAC has provided bombers for service in both Korea and Southeast Asia — the bombers in Korea are under FEAF Bomber Command control, but those in Southeast Asia are under direct SAC control. Beginning in the 1980s some of SAC's bombers have been organized into a Strategic Projection Force (SPF) to provide massive conventional bombing capabilities in support of the Rapid Deployment Force (RDF).

With nearly 105,979 uniformed personnel, SAC is the largest single Major Command in the Air Force. In addition, it is the gaining command for

Above: An airman operates a refueling probe during an aerial refueling such as the one pictured on page one.

Top and right: A B-52, SAC's backbone since the mid-1950's, and a well-guarded B-1B. The massive B-1B will eventually replace the aging B-52.

15,800 members of the Air National Guard and Air Force Reserve. The SAC Force in 1985 was composed of a thousand Minuteman ICBMs (Intercontinental Ballistic Missiles), a handful of Titan ICBMs (now being phased out), 264 Boeing B-52 Stratofortress long-range bombers, 62 General Dynamics FB-111 medium-range bombers and nearly a hundred sophisticated U-2, TR-1 and SR-71 strategic reconnaissance aircraft. In addition, SAC is the sole manager of the Air Force's entire fleet of 615 KC-135 and 25 KC-10 aerial refueling tankers. The first of the new-generation Rockwell B-1B intercontinental bombers were delivered to SAC in 1985, and the first squadron became operational in 1986.

About 30 percent of the bomber and tanker fleet are on a 24-hour ground alert, ready to react immediately in time of war. At the same time, SAC's ICBM force maintains a 24-hour alert posture.

SAC is composed of three major components: the Eighth Air Force, the Fifteenth Air Force, and the First Strategic Aerospace Division. Of the

Bomber pilots and missile 'pilots.' A 93d Bomb Wing B-52G *(above)* and its pilot *(left)* photographed by the author during a low-level training mission. Inside a Titan II Missile complex *(below and bottom)* at Little Rock AFB, Arkansas, Capt James L Daniel, on-site commander *(below)*, clears entry for personnel to enter the complex, and Capt Daniel, First Lt Roy Moore, SMSgt John Herbold and TSgt Raymond A McDaniel perform a trouble analysis as they investigate an equipment malfunction. These missile pilots never see the sky, let alone daylight, when they're on duty in the silos, yet they call their charges 'birds'.

three major strategic air forces of World War II, the Eighth and Fifteenth were both assigned to SAC within six weeks of its creation while the Twentieth, the World War II manager of the B-29 fleet remained a part of that command until permanently disbanded in March 1955.

While there had been a plan in 1970 to eliminate the Eighth Air Force, the plan was changed out of deference to the Eighth's long history, going back to its exploits during World War II in the skies over Germany. The Eighth Air Force instead was re-established on 1 April 1970 at Andersen AFB, Guam, incorporating the Third Air Division, and given jurisdiction over the B-52 *Arc Light* raid against Southeast Asia that originated there. In January 1975, the Eighth was moved back to Barksdale AFB, Louisiana where it replaced the Second Air Force which had been deactivated.

The third component of the present SAC, the First Strategic Aerospace Division (1STRAD), like the numbered air forces, reports directly to SAC headquarters. On 21 July 1961, the former First Missile Division became the first Strategic Aerospace Division based at Vandenberg AFB, California. The original concept called for the First Missile Division to function as the keystone of the SAC ballistic missile force, composed of a diverse conglomeration of missile units based around the country and operating various types of missiles. However, the Thor and Jupiter missiles had been deactivated, and by 1961 the Atlas and Titan units assigned to the First had been transferred to the Fifteenth Air Force.

Thus when the First Strategic Aerospace Division was born, its function was to control the missile test launches taking place at Vandenberg and to train missile crews for SAC. Since 1958 over 1500 launches have taken place at Vandenberg, primarily under the auspices of 1STRAD. These launches have included the huge Titan IIID space booster, many Minuteman launches, and recently the MX test program. As the host unit at Vandenberg, 1STRAD is host to the Air Force's Space and Missile Test Organization, an agency of the Air Force Systems Command (AFSC), conducting missile tests over the Pacific Ocean from its Western Space and Missile Center (WSMC). The WSMC's Western Test Range extends from Vandenberg

The sergeant below is inspecting a turbofan engine. She must have the nicest fingernails on the crew.

A Lockheed SR-71 reconnaissance aircraft photographed by the author at Beale AFB, California as ground crewmen prepared the high-performance plane for a Mach 3 flight to the edge of space. The Blackbird is capable of faster speeds and higher flight than any other aircraft in the world. It s actual top speed has remained a classified secret for twenty years.

across the Pacific and into the Indian Ocean. The Shuttle Activation Task Force (SATAF) at Vandenberg is responsible for supporting the space shuttle as the base becomes its western launch site.

AIR FORCE COMMUNICATIONS COMMAND

The Air Force Communiations Command (AFCC) provides all types of communications support services for the entire Air Force. It is like a seven-fingered communications glove, with each finger covering the needs of a specific Major Command. AFCC's Strategic Communications Division covers the needs of SAC, the Tactical Communications Division covers TAC, the Airlift Communications Division covers MAC, the Space Com-

munications Division covers SPACE-CMD, the European Communications Division covers USAFE and the Pacific Communications Division covers PACAF. The seventh finger in the glove is the Continental Communications Division which covers the other Major Commands and the rest of the Air Force right up to USAF headquarters at the Pentagon. AFCC is headquartered at Scott AFB, Illinois and has permanent facilities at 130 bases but also has a mobile force that can be rapidly deployed anywhere in the world. As of 1985, AFCC had 55,338 personnel, including 7533 civilians, and four aircraft of its own.

While AFCC has seven major divisions, it also provides seven basic services through each: Base Communications (telephone and radio), Inter-Base Communications (radio, cable

A few of the multitude of services the AFCC provides: Sgt Teri Murasso *(left)*, radar repair technician, works on a Precision Cancellor used in the NPM 14 radar unit; Sgt Mark Pitchford *(above)*, member of the Electrical Engineering Group, checks the part number on an integrated circuit before installing it in an ongoing project. AB Michael Reeves *(opposite below)*, telephone switching repair specialist, performs preventative maintenance, and switchboard operators *(below)* at work.

and satellite), Engineering and Installation, Maintenance and Evaluation, Data Automation Systems (computer hardware and software), Air Traffic Control and finally, Combat Communications, which includes mobile C^3 (Command, Control and Communications) and mobile air traffic control under emergency or wartime conditions.

Every time someone lands at an Air Force Base or picks up one of the 650,000 Air Force telephones around the world, he is in the hands of the AFCC. Interbase communications provide the network that really ties the Air Force together. The interbase communications systems include the Automatic Voice Network (AUTOVON), the Automatic Secure Voice Communications Network (AUTOSEVOCOM) and the Automatic Digital Network (AUTODIN). These systems are all part of the Defense Communications System, half of which is leased from commerical communications companies and half of which (including the overseas part) is USAF owned and operated.

AFCC's Air Traffic Control System is the largest military system outside the Soviet Union. AFCC controllers communicate with aircraft under their control from AFB (Air Force Base) towers around the world 35,600 times a day, 365 days a year. When civilian

air traffic controllers walked off their jobs in the summer of 1981, AFCC controllers were loaned to the Federal Aviation Administration (FAA) on an emergency basis and were on duty in commercial towers around the country in a matter of hours. The AFCC controllers fit in quite well at the 65 civilian airports. Despite the fact that AFBs are generally less busy than commercial airports, the traffic is not as strictly scheduled and the controllers have to be on their toes for all types of aircraft making all types of approaches. It is not uncommmon at an Air Force Base for several aircraft to take off simultaneously from the same runway, a rare phenomenon at civilian airports. Air Force controllers also have worked at different bases with different orientation and operations.

AIR FORCE LOGISTICS COMMAND

The mission of the Air Force Logistics Command (AFLC) is to provide combat readiness to the US Air Force. Its job is to buy, transport, supply and maintain virtually all the hardware required to keep the operational commands combat ready. AFSC develops the hardware and AFLC sees that it gets where it's needed and doesn't break down.

AFLC stocks and/or manages nearly 900,000 items and processes nearly five million requisitions annually. It

Top: **Air Force Communications Command air traffic controllers guide military aircraft through crowded skies.**

Above and right: **AFLC personnel stocking fighter tires, and reviewing a schematic drawing at one of the five Air Logistics Centers.**

Opposite: Air Force Logistics Command technicians prepare to run a test on a huge turbofan engine.

Right: A Lockheed F-94 Starfire, which served the US Air Force in the 1950s, undergoes meticulous restoration at the Air Force Museum. The major mission of the Museum is to preserve and restore examples of all the aircraft which have served in the Air Force.

handles not only missiles and aircraft, but nuts, bolts, kitchen sinks and electronic organs for the AFLC Chaplain's Office. So huge are AFLC's logistics operations that it is the largest single-location employer in each of the seven states in which it operates, excluding California. The combined floor space of AFLC's Logistics Centers is significantly larger than the State of Rhode Island. AFLC operates six Logistics Centers—at its headquarters at Wright-Patterson AFB in Ohio, and at McClellen AFB in California, Hill AFB in Washington, Kelly AFB in Texas, Tinker AFB in Oklahoma and Robins AFB in Georgia. In 1985, there were 11,248 military and 85,244 civilian personnel in AFLC.

The US Air Force Museum is AFLC's most publicly visible division. It is also the oldest and largest military aviation museum in the world. Located at Wright-Patterson AFB, Ohio, the Museum has on public display over 200 missiles and aircraft that span the entire history of the USAAS, USAAC, USAAF and USAF. The collections also include historical artifacts and memorabilia of Air Force history. Items from the museum's vast collection also circulate among 20 Air Force base museums around the country as well as 185 other displays and 70 nongovernmental museums in the United States and abroad. The main museum building (large enough to contain a B-36) was completed in 1971 with a major addition completed in 1976.

AIR FORCE SYSTEMS COMMAND

The mission of the Air Force Systems Command (AFSC) is research and development. The AFSC develops and tests the Air Force high-technology hardware in the form of systems ranging from aircraft and avionics to spacecraft and air-to-air missiles. The command also conducts research, development and testing for other Defense Department agencies and NASA. As of 1985, AFSC's 56,254

Right: Whether in lab coat or uniform, AFSC personnel are responsible for USAF systems development.

personnel were equally divided between military (28,654) and civilian (27,600), with two-thirds of the officers holding advanced degrees. AFSC is composed of several divisions (responsible for specific types of systems) and conducts its activities through a nationwide network of laboratories and centers.

The Aeronautical Systems Division (ASD), located at Wright-Patterson AFB, Ohio accounts for over half of AFSC's budget and is responsible for the development of aircraft, engines, aircraft systems, missiles and other airborne systems, as well as flight simulators. The Space Division (SD) is headquartered at Los Angeles AS, California in the heart of a major concentration of space systems contractors and subcontractors. The Space Division has been very closely linked with the Space Command (SPACE-CMD) since the latter's activation in 1983. The commander of AFSC's Space Division is by designation SPACECMD's vice commander. The Space Division manages development of all Department of Defense (DoD) satellites, spacecraft and space systems, and is associated with the NASA Space Shuttle Transportation System. Among the systems within its jurisdiction are communications, meteorological and technology development satellites. Among the Space Division's units are the Air Force Satellite Control Facility (AFSCF) at Sunnyvale AFS, California that operates a global network of satellite-tracking stations, the Manned Space Flight Support Group at the Johnson Space Center near Houston, Texas and the Space and Missile Test Organization (SAMTO) based at SAC's Vandenberg AFB in California. SAMTO manages testing for DoD ballistic missile and space programs, conducting test launches at its two space and missile test centers. The Western Space and Missile Test Center (WSMC) is located at Vandenberg AFB with a western test range stretching across the Pacific into the Indian Ocean. WSMC conducts polar-orbit space-launch operations, ballistic missile tests in conjunction with SAC, and effective 1986, Space Shuttle operations. The Eastern Space and Missile Center (ESMC) operates from Patrick AFB and Cape Canaveral AFS in Florida, the primary

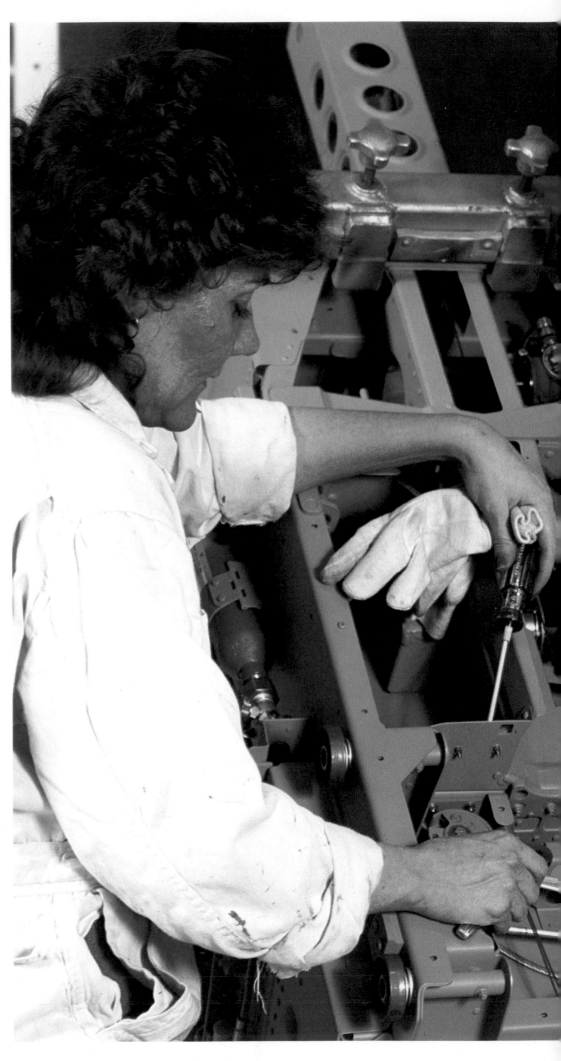

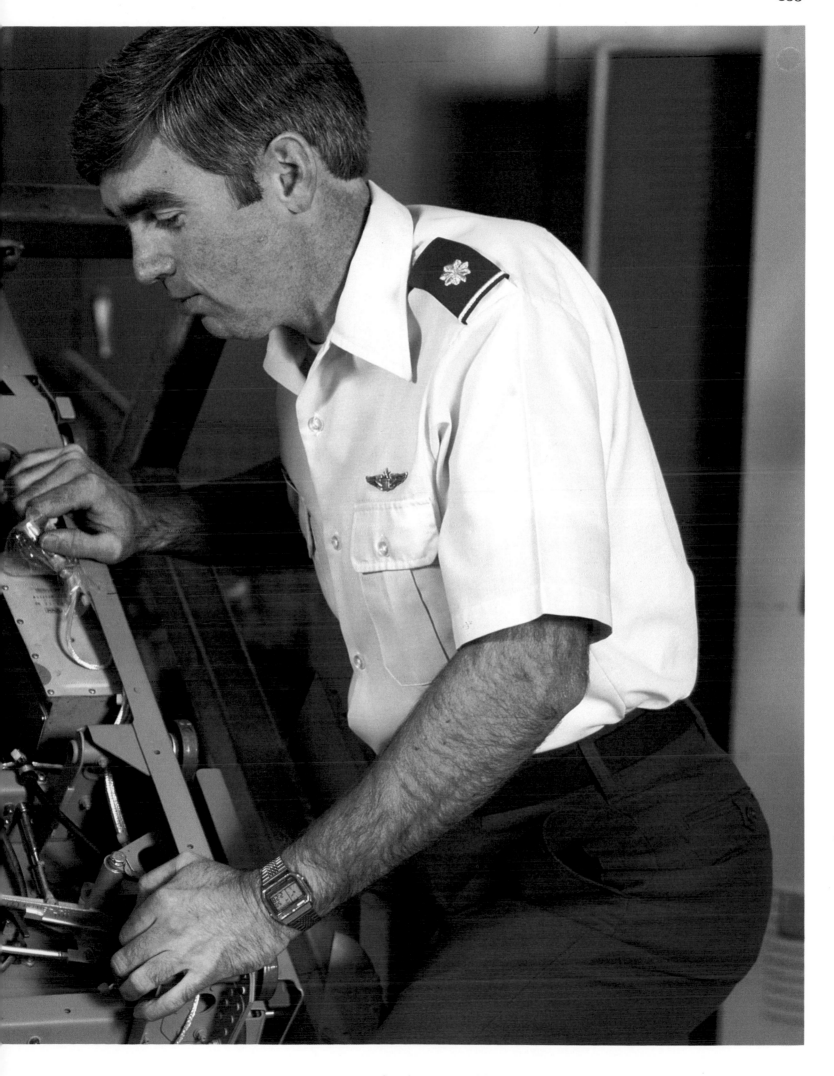

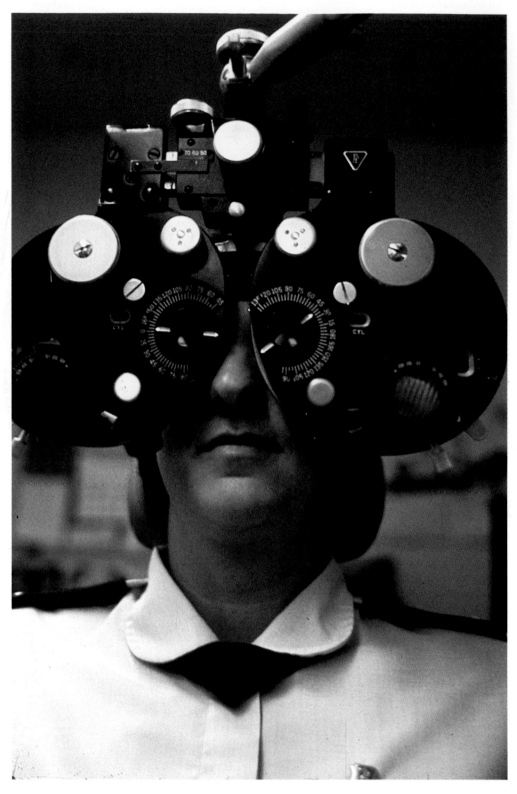

The Air Force Systems Command conducts health care research *(left)* at the Aerospace Medical Division, as well as monitoring development of aircraft and helicopters.

test field for over 50 years, starting back when the Air Force was still the Air Corps. Located on California's Mojave Desert, it has one of the largest ground complexes in the world with 15,000 square miles of unrestricted airspace. The main runway measures 15,000 feet but two dry lake beds provide a 40,000-foot runway for landing any type of research aircraft. Near-perfect flying weather and a semi-isolated location combine to provide a safe and secure environment for flight test operations. Edwards provided the ideal landing site for the early Space Shuttle flights. The center plans, conducts and evaluates manned and unmanned aircraft and spacecraft for the Air Force, NASA and other agencies. Practically every aircraft that has become operational with the Air Force, and many research aircraft that never became operational, first went through their paces at Edwards.

The Arnold Enginering Development Center (AEDC) at Arnold AFS, Tennessee must ensure that aerospace hardware, whether aircraft, spacecraft, missiles or propulsion systems, work right the first time they fly. Virtually every major American aerospace system has been supported by tests conducted at AEDC. Clients of AEDC include not only the Air Force, but NASA, the other services and aerospace industry contractors as well. The Center operates the largest and most advanced complex of flight simulation test facilities in the world.

The Armament Division (AD) of AFSC and its Air Force Armament Test Laboratory (AFATL) both located at Eglin AFB, Florida develop, test and procure all of the Air Force's non-nuclear air weapons and related equipment. These weapons and equipment include air-launched tactical and defense missiles, guided weapons, aircraft guns and ammunition, targets and related armament support equipment.

The Aerospace Medical Division (AMD) of AFSC, based at Brooks AFB, Texas conducts research and development in flight medicine, environmental health, biomedical education and epidemiology. The Foreign Technology Division (FTD), based at Wright-Patterson AFB, Ohio collects, evaluates and

Space Shuttle launch site, with tracking and data-gathering stations on the islands of Grand Bahama, Grand Turk, Antigua and Ascension. The Eastern Test Range extends across the Atlantic, and like the Western Test Range, into the Indian Ocean as well.

The Ballistic Missile Office (BMO) is headquartered at MAC's Norton AFB in California and is responsible for planning, implementation and management of USAF ballistic missile system and subsystem programs. The Electronic Systems Division (ESD), headquartered at Hanscom AFB, Mas-

sachusetts is the primary USAF agency for the development and acquisition of command, control, communications and intelligence (C^3I) systems. These systems include radar and optical detection systems, used to locate and track aircraft, satellites and missiles, that range from SPACECMD's radar network to TAC's E-3A AWACS electronic reconnaissance aircraft.

The Air Force Flight Test Center (AFFTC) at Edwards AFB, California is probably the most well known of AFSC's bases and centers. It has served as the Air Force's primary flight

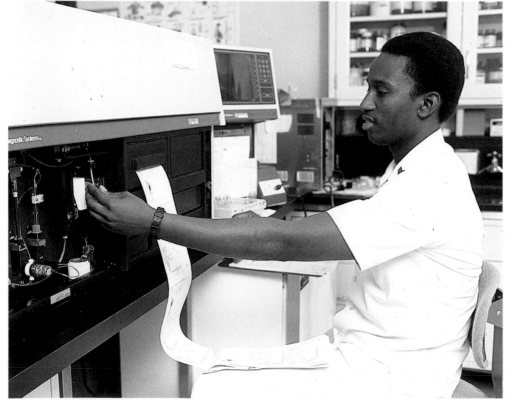

Technical hardware for the Air Force mission may include a KC-135 simulator such as this one 'flown' by Lts Dale Hawthorne and Julie Tizard *(above)*, a medical diagnostic computer *(left)*, an EF-111 Raven electronic warfare aircraft *(opposite top)* or the antenna being installed *(opposite bottom)* by Sgt Joey Balay atop an EMC van.

analyzes information about foreign aerospace technology. FTD works with other divisions of AFSC in the collection and evaluation of data. The result is an assessment of the potential effects that foreign developments may have on USAF operations. The Air Force Contract Management Division (AFCMD), located at Kirtland AFB, New Mexico administers DoD aerospace contracts for the Air Force, the other services and NASA. Finally, there is AFSC's Directorate of Laboratories, an office that monitors and directs a network of AFSC laboratories around the country at both AFSC and non-AFSC bases.

ELECTRONIC SECURITY COMMAND

The Electronic Security Command (ESC), headquartered at Kelly AFB near San Antonio, Texas is the USAF's electronic warfare command. A Major Command in its present form since August 1979, ESC's forerunner was the US Air Force Security Service (USAFSS) formed in October 1948. USAFSS began with 11 officers and five enlisted men.

In 1979 USAFSS was deactivated and ESC formed. In 1985 there were 12,723 military and 1009 civilian personnel in ESC.

While the mission of AFCC is to communicate (C^3), the mission of today's ESC is to develop an offensive capability in Electronic Countermeasures in order to jam, confuse or destroy the enemy's C^3 (this is C^3 Countermeasures or C^3CM), and prevent him from activating his own C^3CM against Amer-

ican C^3 and C^3CM. ESC, like AFCC, has divisions that operate with USAF combat Commands.

Since 1981 realistic Electronic Warfare (EW) training has been provided through the *Green Flag* exercises sometimes held in conjunction with TAC's *Red Flag* exercises at Nellis AFB, Nevada. Complex computer models are used to test both the hardware and the tactics of electronic warfare. Today the primary Air Force EW/ECM tactical jamming aircraft is the Grumman EF-111A, based on the General Dynamics F-111 tactical fighter. The EF-111 is designed for close-in jamming operations, stand-off jamming operations and for escorting attack aircraft penetrating enemy airspace, such as the old EB-66 did over Vietnam. Its equipment includes the internally mounted ALQ-99 primary jammer, ALQ-137/ALR-62 self-protection systems and provision for carrying the new ALQ-131 externally. Augmenting the 42 EF-

Left: Airman First Class Richard Bogvett directs a 60th Airlift Wing C-141 to a parking place at Biggs Army Air Field near El Paso, Texas. In April 1985, both Air Force and Army units participated in a joint readiness exercise called *Border Star 85.* The Military Airlift Command provided tactical airlift and redeployment support to the exercise, and was photographed in action by SMSgt Don Sutherland and SSgt Michael Haggerty.

Below: A 63d Military Airlift Wing C-141, photographed by the author on completion of an early evening landing at Andrews AFB near Washington, DC. A Military Airlift Command base, Andrews is the aerial gateway to the nation's capital for official air operations. The 89th Military Airlift Wing, which includes *Air Force One,* is based at Andrews AFB.

111s are the EC-130H *Compass Call* aircraft which are designed to perform stand-off jamming, disrupting enemy C^3 over large areas of the battlefront.

In addition to its manned airborne systems, ESC also has both remotely piloted EW drone aircraft and ground-based systems. All of these systems, and many even more sophisticated than those now publicly known, are being developed; electronic warfare, along with C^3CM will be an integral part of the battlefield environment in any future war. On the battlefield of the future, events will move with startling speed, and destructive force will be tied together by an intricate web of C^3, which the opposing force will try to disrupt. On that battlefield, disruption of an enemy's C^3 could theoretically mean the defeat of that enemy.

MILITARY AIRLIFT COMMAND

In the early days of the USAAS and USAAC when the aircraft were of short range and modest speed, most of those services' own supplies and personnel moved from base to base by train. Flying was generally something you went to the base to do, not a means of getting to the base. World War II changed this. By the 1940s civilian transports had evolved into aircraft that could carry large numbers of people, not just a couple of hardy souls. General Hap Arnold called World War II a war of logistics, and an important part of logistical transport was by air. From a prewar airlift capacity of practically nil the USAAF developed an extensive system serving land forces as well as its own needs that would be a model of post-war military airlift.

Since the war the Military Airlift Command (MAC) has continued to be the prime agent for global airlift in the US Air Force and in the entire US defense establishment. Until 1965, the Major Theater Commands had their own short-range tactical airlift wings, but as of March of that year, all tactical and aeromedical intra-theater airlift resources in the USAF were assigned to MAC.

MAC is headquartered at Scott AFB, Illinois and is composed of three numbered air forces. The 21st Air Force out of McGuire AFB, New Jersey, controls airlift operations eastward through Canada, Greenland, Iceland, NATO Europe, Africa and the Middle East,

Left: SSgt Allen Barrie, a MAC C-130 loadmaster from Norton AFB, computes a mission load plan.

Right: MAC airlift action includes checking a medevac patient *(top),* or TSgt Ray Harris tying down bundles in a C-130E.

and southward into the Caribbean and South America. The 22d Air Force out of Travis AFB, California controls airlift operations in the entire Pacific area, Antarctica, Diego Garcia and westward to the Arabian Peninsula where its area meets that of the 21st. The 23d Air Force is based at MAC headquarters, Scott AFB. It has no geographic boundary and is the focal point of MAC Special Operations and the Aerospace Rescue and Recovery Service (ARRS).

The Aerospace Rescue and Recovery Service was born as the Air Rescue Service (ARS) in December 1946 with the mission to conduct search and rescue missions to save downed pilots. The ARS (ARRS since 8 January 1966) was responsible for saving numerous pilots in both Korea and Southeast Asia, with many of the rescues taking place under enemy fire. ARS and ARRS have also played a key role in the recovery of capsules of the manned spaceflight program. ARRS operates a fleet of about 200 airplanes and helicopters, including UH/HH-1s, CH/HH-3s, CH/HH-53s and various types of C-130s. In addition to rescuing downed pilots, ARRS has participated with other MAC units in global humanitarian airlift operations such as the October 1980 operation in which ARRS saved 65 people from the sinking civilian cruise ship *Prinsendam* in the Gulf of Alaska.

Global humanitarian airlift is a MAC tradition that goes back to the Berlin Airlift. In time of disaster MAC is on hand to deliver food and medical supplies and to evacuate the wounded and refugees. Among some of the highlights are operations that span the globe and MAC history. In 1973, MAC evacuated a hospital in Iceland endangered by an exploding volcano. In Operation *Sno-Go* in February 1977, MAC airlifted two million pounds of snowplows and 600 relief workers to the Buffalo, New York area in the wake of what was called the 'Blizzard of the Century.' In March 1979 MAC airlifted a 115-ton water filtration system and other equipment to Harrisburg, Pennsylvania after the nuclear power plant

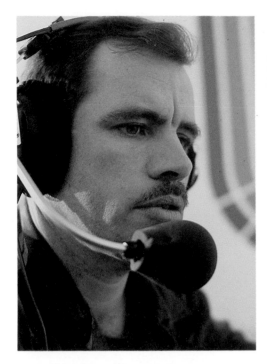

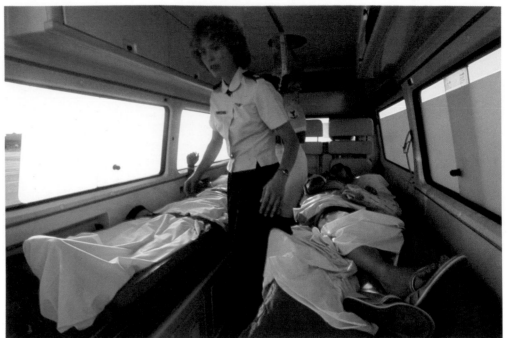

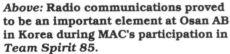

Above: **Radio communications proved to be an important element at Osan AB in Korea during MAC's participation in** *Team Spirit 85.*

Counterclockwise from above right: **On 25 July 1985, Captain Vera Brown of MAC's 2d Aeromedical Evacuation Squadron was dispatched from Rhein Main AB to Sigonella NAS, in Sicily to pick up a patient with a possible appendicitis. She was assisted by a US Navy ambulance driver and Sgt Wayne Brown of the 2d AES** *(right).* **During the medevac flight (in a MAC 2d AES C-9) Captain Brown administered Polycillin-N. The airlift, photographed by SSgt Fernando Serna, was all in a day's work for the 2d AES.**

Far right: **SSgt David Licht, photographed by MSgt Ken Hammond at Andrews AFB, is a ground crew chief assigned to MAC's First Helicopter Squadron.**

Bottom: **A C-141B Starlifter transport catches the last rays of a setting sun at Andrews AFB.**

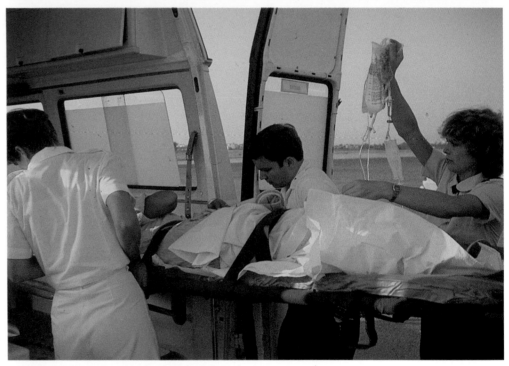

emergency at Three Mile Island. In May 1980, when Mount St Helens erupted in Washington State, MAC provided communications and rescue services, saving 61 lives. In addition to these unique operations, MAC planes and helicopters have airlifted aid to victims of typhoons, floods, earthquakes and other natural disasters in countries on every continent from Peru to Yugoslavia and from Alaska to Iran.

MAC's Air Weather Service (AWS) headquartered at Scott AFB, Illinois operates a network of weather observation and forecasting facilities to support Army and Air Force units all over the world. AWS works with ARRS in the area of tropical-storm reconnaissance as well as providing weather

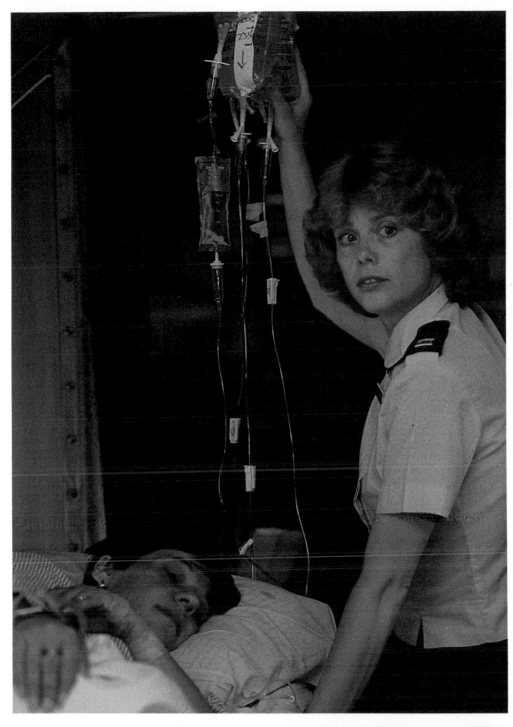

forecasts prior to aircraft deployments, missile and satellite launches and other military operations.

MAC is a military command, but by the nature of its mission it is much like a civilian airline. It has an established worldwide route structure serving 21 *inter-theater* aerial ports and 22 *intra-theatre* operating locations, with commercial gateway operating locations (OL) at 13 major commercial airports around the world. MAC also has regular passenger and cargo schedules and provides executive transport for members of the legislative and executive branches of the federal government (including the president) through the 89th Military Airlift (of the 21st Air Force) based at Andrews AFB outside Washington DC.

One of the two major components of MAC's 23d Air Force — along with the ARRS — is the MAC Second Air Division, based at TAC's Hurlburt Field, Florida with a detachment at Howard AFB in Panama. The Second Air Division contains the First Special Operations Wings at Hurlburt Field, the First Special Operations Squadron based at Clark AB in the Philippines and the Seventh Special Operations Squadron at Rhein-Main AB in Germany. The Second Air Division is the US Air Force's commando team, conducting 'special operations' such as unconventional warfare operations. The Second Air Division was created in the wake of the disastrous attempt to rescue American hostages in Iran in 1980. Its aircraft include HH-53 and UH-1N helicopters, MC-130 transports and the AC-130 Spectre gunships

Above: MAC helicopter rescue operations in Korea during the *Team Spirit 84* exercise included suppressing 'enemy' ground fire *(left)*, while a 'wounded' man was reeled in *(right)*.

Below: TSgt James Derrick stands guard during the *Solid Shield 85* exercise at Ft Stewart, Georgia, waiting for 'wounded' to be loaded into the waiting HH-3 Jolly Green Giant.

Right: Military Airlift Command personnel, such as this airman photographed by Sgt Gus Garcia at Luxembourg Airport during *Reforger 84*, take part in joint readiness exercises worldwide.

born in Vietnam. By 1982 infra-red-equipped Spectres were flying night-time surveillance missions over war-torn El Salvador from Howard AFB, Panama.

The Second Air Division works in close conjunction with the elite commandos of the other services such as the Army's Green Berets and the Navy's SEALS (Sea/Air/Land). It provides their airlift capability and assists them in operations such as *Urgent Fury* of October 1983.

As of 1985, there were 821 transport aircraft in the US Air Force. Over 700 are the three major types that make up the backbone of MAC's airlift fleet. Informally classed as 'medium,' 'large,' and 'extra-large,' these aircraft are all built by Lockheed. For medium-range intratheater hauling under adverse conditions or into semi-improved landing strips, there were 360 C-130

Above: The Lockheed C-140 Jetstar is an executive-type jet that MAC uses for short hops, such as to carry small numbers of personnel from base to base in the United States.

Below: The Lockheed C-141B Starlifter is the backbone of MAC's worldwide airlift mission. All 268 of them used to be C-141As, but they have been modified to carry larger loads through a 23 foot lengthening of their fuselages. Only MAC's huge C-5 Galaxy can carry a larger load than the Starlifter.

Above right: SSgt Victor Rodriguez, a flight engineer with MAC's 37th Tactical Airlift Squadron, checks the wing fuel tank of a C-130E before takeoff from Aviano AB in Italy during an Operational Readiness Inspection in November 1984. SSgt Rodriguez is probably familiar with the old joke about the match and the gas tank. The exercise was photographed by TSgt Jose Lopez and Sgt Glenda Pellum.

Right: From his station in the right side of the cockpit, a C-141 flight engineer can monitor all of the aircraft's systems in flight.

The Lockheed C-130 Hercules *(above)* **provides MAC with the ability to airlift materiel to virtually any type of airfield; while huge C-5 Galaxies, such as these photographed by the author at Travis AFB** *(left)***, can carry very large loads over intercontinental distances.**

Hercules aircraft (average age of 17 years). For large loads carried over long distances, there were 271 C-141 Starlifters (average age of 18 years), and for extremely large loads, such as the US Army's main battle tanks, there were 77 C-5 Galaxies (average age of 13 years), the largest fully operational aircraft in the world. The C-130 production line was still humming and the Galaxy was back in production with the improved C-5B. At the same time, the Air Force was in the process of working with McDonnell Douglas to develop the C-17 airlifter, which could carry those oversize items presently carried only by the C-5 and carry them just as far. However, it could also land on just about any level patch of ground, a special capability of the workhorse C-130.

Other noteworthy transports in the US Air Force fleet include 25 McDonnell Douglas C-9 Nightingale medical evacuation hospital planes (average age of 14 years) and 59 Beechcraft C-12 Super Kings (average age of 4 years). These small general aviation-type aircraft are used to transport overseas air attachés and advisors. Other general aviation-type aircraft in service with MAC in 1985 were 12 Lockheed C-140 Jet Stars and 115 Rockwell C7-39 Sabreliners. The average age of both types was 22 years and they both were being phased out. Their replacements were the Grumman C-20 Gulfstream and the Gates Learjet C-21 which began entering service in 1983 with planned final totals of 11 and 80 units respectively.

SPACE COMMAND

It was against the background of an increasing realization of the strategic importance of space that the US Air Force Space Command (SPACECMD) came into being on 1 September 1982. The new Major Command took as its headquarters Peterson AFB in Colorado in addition to Clear AFS in Alaska and Thule AB and Sondrestrom AB in Greenland. The TAC Aerospace Defense Center commander, General James Hartinger, was redesignated as SPACECMD's first commander.

Peterson AFB comprises 1176 acres at an altitude of 6200 feet in the Colorado Rockies, seven miles east of Colorado Springs. The centerpiece of Peterson AFB is the Cheyenne Mountain Complex, buried 1700 feet in the solid granite of the mountain. It contains the control center and headquarters of SPACECMD (and formerly ADC) as well as the North American Air Defense Command (NORAD). In the late 1950s the joint US-Canada NORAD Command decided on the need for an impregnable underground com-

The US Air Force Space Command personnel in action: guarding the Space Shuttle at Vandenberg AFB *(opposite)*, practicing a rescue from a Space Shuttle simulator at Patrick AFB *(right)*, tracking an Air Force satellite as it orbits the earth *(above, right)* and guarding America's horizons from the PAVE PAWS radar site at Beale AFB *(top)*.

Left: **A California Air National Guard F-106 Delta Dagger, its tail marked with the state's golden bear, fires an AIM-4.**

Above: **Airmen of the Colorado Air National Guard unload disaster relief medical supplies flown by a Special Air Mission to Khartoum in the Sudan.**

mand center that could be protected from enemy nuclear attack. Cheyenne Mountain was selected. Originally designed to track bombers, the Cheyenne Mountain Complex today still houses the Aerospace Defense Center, to which has been added SPACECMD's Space Defense Operations Center (SPADOC). SPADOC not only tracks satellites and spacecraft, but serves as a space-intelligence clearinghouse and space-operations command post as well. The new Consolidated Space Operations Center (CSOC) is located nine miles away at Falcon AFS. From the CSOC, SPACECMD controls operational spacecraft and also plans, manages and controls all Defense Department space shuttle flights.

The creation of SPACECMD was inevitable, given the level of Soviet activity in space and the growing need to protect Air Force communications and reconnaissance satellites. SPACECMD will be the the Air Force's operational space force but has also been assigned to promote a closer relationship between the research and development community and operational units. The mission of the Air Force's newest command is far reaching. Its potential equals that of the former USAAF. It is possible that SPACECMD may one day form the basis of a separate military service.

AIR TRAINING COMMAND

The Air Training Command (ATC) is headquartered at Randolph AFB near San Antonio, Texas with bases throughout the United States. It is its job to recruit and train the men and women in Air Force blue. To fulfill this mission ATC operates the largest school system in the free world with 1250 admissions offices and more than 3000 course offerings. In 1985 there were 14,043 civilian and 70,738 military personnel (including permanent personnel and students) assigned to ATC. In 1984 ATC trained 2305 pilots and 1195 navigators including 160 foreign pilots, 26 foreign navigators and 217 US Navy and Marine Corps navigators. ATC is responsible not only for flying training, but technical training, recruiting, basic military training, professional military training and specialized education as well.

Outside of the 3300 tactical aircraft assigned to ATC and the tactical theater commands, there are more aircraft assigned to ATC than to any other com-

mand. Of the 1708 trainers in the US Air Force in 1985, 615 of them were Cessna T-37 Dragonflys, ATC's standard primary trainer (average age of 22 years) and 820 of them were Northrop T-38 Talons, ATC's standard advanced trainer (average age of 19 years). Both are twin-engine, two-seat aircraft. Other trainers in the ATC inventory include the 27-year-old Lockheed T-33 T-Bird, the Air Force's original jet trainer, of which an amazing 114 were still in service in 1985. ATC's largest trainer is the Boeing T-43 which is the military version of the Boeing 737 jetliner. Between 1973 and 1974, 19 of these aircraft were acquired for use as navigational trainers. The next-generation trainer is the Fairchild Republic T-46, which began to replace the T-37 in 1985.

A more thorough examination of the workings of ATC, as well as of the Air Force Academy and the Air University begin on page 87.

AIR GUARD AND RESERVES

Together, the Air National Guard (ANG) and the Air Force Reserve (AFRES) compose America's 'shadow air force,' a pool of trained reserve personnel who can be called up to augment the regular Air Force in time of crisis, national emergency or war. AFRES is a Separate Operating Agency of the US Air Force. However, Air National Guard (known familarly as the 'Air Guard'), like the (Army) National Guard, is under the command of the governors of each of the fifty states, Puerto Rico, Guam, the Virgin Islands, and of the

commanding general for the District of Columbia. A governor may call up elements of the National Guard to protect lives in time of natural disaster and civil unrest. Hardly a winter storm season goes by without scenes of an ANG helicopter rescuing someone from a rooftop somewhere in the country. In time of war the president may 'nationalize' the National Guard, at which time they join the regular Army and regular Air Force units overseas.

The Air Force Reserve (AFRES) has the mission of training reserve Air Force personnel to be ready for mobilization. The manpower administration support required for the mobilization of the AFRES is provided by the Air Reserve Personnel Center in Denver, Colorado which is now also a Separate Operating Agency (SOA). Reservists are part-time personnel or the 'weekend warriors' of the Air Force. AFRES is headquartered at Robins AFB, Georgia and organized into three (formerly ADC active-duty) numbered air forces.

Like the ANG, AFRES participates in many annual readiness exercises including *Reforger* in Europe, *Brim Frost* in Alaska, *Team Spirit* in the Pacific and *Red Flag*. The AFRES crews and units assigned to MAC are constantly present on MAC's global airlift routes. AFRES units constitute 10 percent of Air Force fighter squadrons and are consistently represented among top units in fighter-weapons competitions.

Like the Air Guard, the Reserve has generally received aircraft that has been in service for awhile with the regular Air Force. This situation, however, is changing. Beginning in 1981 with the introduction into SAC of the new McDonnell Douglas KC-10 Extender aerial-refueling tanker, the AFRES was designated to supply 50 percent of the crews. The tanker is identical in almost all respects (save for the aerial-refueling systems) to the commercial DC-10 jetliner, and many of the AFRES pilots have regular jobs flying DC-10s for the airlines. AFRES units are also receiving A-10s at the same time as regular Air Force units and are receiving 'factory fresh' C-130s. Because of their long-term training and prior service, the Reservists and the Guardsmen are often called the best reserve air force in the world. The AFRES and the ANG provide a highly competent and highly economical backup to the regular Air Force.

Above: **Airman Lee Nupson and TSgt Carl Moyer of the Minnesota Air Guard replace a hydraulic seal on a C-130 prop during *Reforger 84* in Germany.**

Far right: **Rest time for the Louisiana Air National Guard at the Suwon AB, Korea tent city during the *Team Spirit 85* exercise.**

JOINING THE PEOPLE IN AIR FORCE BLUE

The Air Training Command (ATC) is known in the Air Force as the 'First Command' because anyone bound for any destination on the Air Force career ladder stops there first. The people who arrive at that first rung come from three principal sources: the Air Force Recuiting Service; various school programs such as the Air Force Reserve Officer Training Corps at colleges and universities around the United States; and the US Air Force Academy. The first two sources are part of the Air Training Command, while the Academy is an independent Direct Reporting Unit.

The US Air Force Recruiting Service (USAFRS) is, like ATC itself, headquartered at Randolph AFB, Texas. Established in 1959, USAFRS monitors the activities of five recruiting groups (based in California, Georgia, Illinois, Massachusetts and Texas), 40 recruiting squadrons, 1250 recruiting offices and 1800 individual recruiters throughout the United States, Puerto Rico and Guam. About 800 recruiters are also stationed near concentrations of Americans overseas in Japan, the Philippines, West Germany and the United Kingdom. The USAFRS Directorate of Health Professions Recruit-

Opposite: A US Air Force Academy cadet, saber at the ready.

Above: Lt Gomes beside the T-38 in which she'll train for supersonic flight.

ing, established in 1973, has 35 medical recruiting teams whose job is to recruit doctors, dentists and nurses for service in the Air Force.

In 1984 the USAFRS recruited nearly 65,000 officers and airmen including 1013 healthcare professionals. Of these, 2686 were college graduates, with a mean grade point average of 3.12, who went directly into ATC's Officer Training School (OTS). While 1984 was not a typical year for USAFRS —because it was their best to date— the demographics give a good idea of the type of people the Service recruits. Of the 1984 group, 99 percent were high school graduates, 20 percent had 15 or more hours of college credit and 51 percent scored in the top two categories on their qualifying tests.

Through the Air Force Reserve Officer Training Corps (AFROTC), ATC starts to train certain specialized volunteers for future careers as Air Force officers while the candidates are still in colleges and universities. The AFROTC program offers four-year on-campus training to students enrolled in 746 colleges and universities through 150 AFROTC detachments. Of the students enrolled in the AFROTC program, an average of 10 per school receive

AFROTC scholarships. Under the program, AFROTC enrollees are commissioned as USAF second lieutenants upon graduation, the number usually averaging about 3200 per year.

AFROTC also offers a Junior ROTC (JROTC) program providing aerospace education to approximately 40,000 students at 286 American high schools in the United States and overseas. Graduates with JROTC backgrounds are able to enlist in the Air Force with the rank of airman first class.

The College Senior Engineer Program is another way qualified individuals may enter the Air Force. Applicants may be college juniors and seniors majoring in aeronautical, aerospace, architectural, astronautical, electrical, or nuclear engineering. Those who qualify are enlisted as airmen first class with full pay and fringe benefits and are promoted to staff sergeant upon graduation. After graduation they are assigned to ATC's three-month Officer Training School, and upon completion of OTS they are commissioned as second lieutenants.

AIR FORCE TRAINING

Once recruited, new enlisted personnel report to Lackland AFB, Texas for a six-week basic military training program that also includes academic training, physical conditioning and marksmanship. The Officer Training School, also at Lackland, prepares selected college graduates and college-educated enlisted personnel to be USAF officers. The OTS program includes both military and academic training as well as marksmanship and physical training. Students scheduled for pilot training enter a three-week flight screening program conducted in T-41 Mescaleros.

Work details are still as much a part of Air Force basic training as they were in grandfather's day. The fact that the dining halls at Lackland AFB have been contractor-operated since 1974 has not meant an end to traditional KP, though the kitchen police of grandfather's day are now called mess attendants. The contractors are responsible for cooking and serving the meals, but the Air Force recruits still unload the trucks, wash the dishes and scrub the floors.

Technical training is conducted at five Air Training Command Technical Training Centers: Keesler AFB in Mississippi, Chanute AFB in Illinois,

Top: KP certainly is more an art than it once was, if this photo by SMSgt Buster Kellum of three airmen preparing some rather appetizing salads is any sort of indication.

Above and opposite: Three airmen, ATC patches prominent on their uniforms, examine a jet engine model, while an ATC instructor works with a lieutenant aboard a T-43 navigation trainer.

homa; and Williams AFB, Arizona; with pilot instructor training conducted at Randolph AFB, Texas. Senior cadets at the Air Force Academy take part in an Indoctrination Program in the T-41 conducted by the 557th Flying Training Wing.

Beginning in 1988 ATC will introduce Specialized Undergraduate Pilot Training (SUPT). In SUPT, all flight trainees will have the same primary training to learn fundamental flying skills, but will then enter one of two different training tracks. These will be the Fighter/Attack/Reconnaissance (FAR) track which will continue to use the T-38 as its trainer, or the Tanker/Transport/Bomber (TTB) track which will use another trainer with a larger flight deck, probably an existing multi-engine business jet.

Navigator training is a 28-week undergraduate program conducted only at Mather AFB in California. The ground instruction covers airmanship; basic navigation procedures and equipment; celestial, radar and low-altitude environment navigation; map reading and weather. Undergraduate navigator flying training is conducted aboard T-37s and T-43s.

Graduate courses offered by ATC at Mather include a 4-week advanced navigation program, a 5-week tactical navigation program, a 14-week navigator-bombardier program and a 21-week electronic warfare training program. In addition to the graduate and undergraduate courses, four specialized programs are offered: electronic warfare operations and staff officer training, senior officer electronic warfare training, electronic warfare refresher training, and an electronic warfare course for US Army air defense officers.

Basic survival training is given annually to about 5000 aircrew members at Fairchild AFB, Washington with a water survival course given at Homestead AFB, Florida and an arctic survival course given at Eielson AFB in Alaska. ATC also monitors survival training conducted by the Air Force Academy and by AFSC's School of Aerospace Medicine at Brooks AFB in Texas. The ATC Environmental Information Division at Maxwell AFB, Alabama collects, evaluates and publishes data on natural and cultural environments that are potentially pertinent to survival and life support training.

The Defense Language Institute

Lowrey AFB in Colorado, Sheppard AFB in Texas and Goodfellow AFB in Texas. An additional 90 field locations are used as well. Technical training is an ongoing process that continues throughout a person's Air Force career, with 300,000 students graduating annually from more than 2800 formal training courses. The courses include supply services, personnel, medical services, maintenance and communications, computer operations and, of course, aircraft and missile systems operation.

Pilot training in ATC is a 49-week undergraduate program conducted for officers selected to become pilots. Training includes 500 hours of ground instruction and 175 hours of flying— 74 in the T-37 jet trainer and 101 in the Supersonic T-38. The undergraduate pilot training is conducted at Columbus AFB, Mississippi; Laughlin AFB, Texas; Reese AFB, Texas; Vance AFB, Okla-

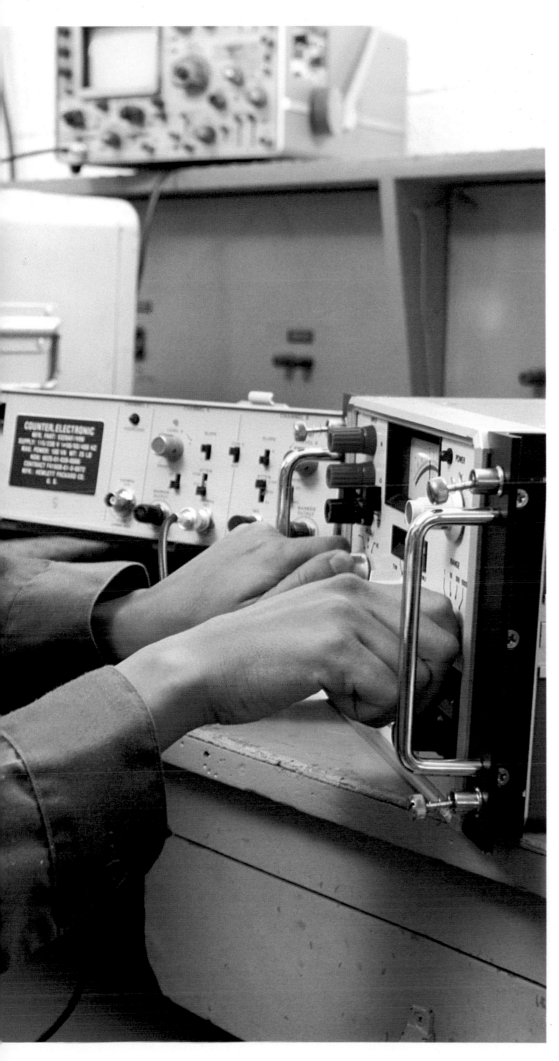

Left: **Electronics has always been an extremely important element in the Air Training Command curriculum, as it is in the Air Force itself.**

English Language Center at Lackland AFB in Texas conducts English language training programs for the Department of Defense. The 3500 students that annually attend the Center are mostly military officers from 41 countries in Europe, Africa, Asia, the Middle East and Latin America who are being trained in the United States. Some will eventually receive ATC pilot training. The average course is 16 weeks, but can range from 4 weeks to a year. The center also provides a 27-week English language instructor course and a 13-week advanced instructor course to foreign students.

The Civil Air Patrol is a civilian volunteer organization, headed by a USAF officer selected by the secretary of the Air Force, that became an official auxiliary of the USAF in 1948. Its services include air search and rescue operations and other emergency operations, communications, and youth motivation through aerospace education and leadership training.

The Community College of the Air Force was established in 1972 at Maxwell AFB, Alabama. The College provides both on- and off-duty academic and technical education for enlisted personnel at locations throughout the Air Force. The College is accredited by the Southern Association of Colleges and the School's Commission on Colleges. It is the only federal agency with the authority to award associate degrees.

In 1980 ATC became the host of the EURO-NATO Joint Jet Pilot Training (ENJJPT) Program. The 55-week NATO-sponsored training program takes place at Sheppard AFB in Texas and is very similar to the West German Luftwaffe under-graduate training program that was formerly conducted at Sheppard. The Luftwaffe is again represented in ENJJPT, as well as fighter pilot trainees from the air forces of Belgium, Canada, Denmark, Greece, Holland, Norway, Portugal, Turkey and the United Kingdom. The course involves 452 classroom hours in 17 academic courses, and 216 flying training days. The flying training includes 110.6 hours of flying time, with 26.4 solo hours in the T-38. The number of students in the program will reach a maximum of 254 in 1985 with a ratio of 144 foreign to 110 USAF personnel.

THE US AIR FORCE ACADEMY

When the independent US Air Force was created in 1947, many of its leaders, who had come up through the ranks of the US Army and many of them via its Military Academy at West Point, recognized the need for an Air Force Academy. Established by Act of Congress, signed into law by President Dwight Eisenhower on 1 April 1954, the Air Force Academy became the newest service academy as it joined West Point, the Naval Academy and the Coast Guard Academy. With the establishment of the Academy authorized, Secretary of the Air Force Harold Talbott appointed a commis-

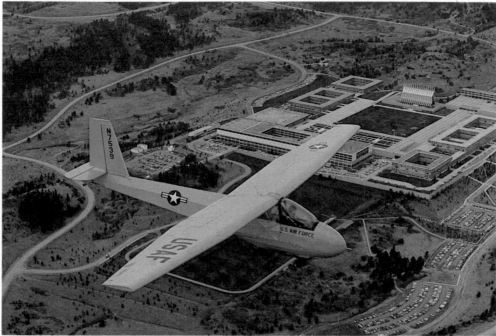

"BRING ME MEN"

Portraits of the US Air Force Academy. An honor guard drills before the Academy's distinctive chapel (above, left); new cadets arrive on the grounds, duffle bags in hand (opposite); one of the Academy's gliders in flight over the campus (top right); and a graduating class, men and women included, marching proudly toward their careers in the US Air Force (above, right).

sion to help him select a permanent site. The commission considered 580 sites in 45 states, narrowing these prospective locations to three, from which Talbott selected one near Colorado Springs, Colorado. The first Air Force Academy class began their academic career in temporary facilities at Lowry AFB in Denver in July 1958 as

construction began on the Academy campus. The cadet wing made its move to the nearly complete campus in August 1958, and the first class of 207 graduates was commissioned as second lieutenants in June 1959. The Academy's degree program had already been accredited by the Commission of Colleges and Universities of the North Central Association of Colleges and Secondary Schools.

Among the elements of cadet training are professional military studies, military training, leadership, aviation science and flight training in gliders as well as T-43 and T-41 aircraft. The cadet honor code is 'We will not lie, steal, cheat, nor tolerate among us anyone who does.'

Naturally, parachuting or sky-diving can be expected to be part of the training program at the Academy. The school's parachute demonstration team, Wings of Blue, competes annually in intercollegiate competitions, winning first place in the 40-school national competition nearly every year since they became involved. In addition to the competitions, Wings of Blue puts on about 40 public demonstrations each year.

One of the more interesting extracurricular activities on campus is falconry. The mascot of the Academy's athletic teams is the 'Fighting Falcon,' officially represented by a gyrfalcon named Glacier, who is an integral part of many Air Force Academy functions.

Below: The Strategic Air Command's KC-10 Extender is an aerial refueling aircraft based on the DC-10 jetliner. It carries 356,065 lb of aviation fuel, much more than earlier tankers.

INDEX

A-4 Skyhawk 280, *280, 284-285*
A-6E Intruder 109, 143, 219, *275, 280*
A-7 Corsair *130*, 312
A-10 Thunderbolt 312, *315*, 336, 338
A-37 Dragonfly 312, *313*
Achille Lauro incident 188
Adams, President John 203, 206, 263
Aerospace Defense Command (ADCOM) 313
Aerospace Rescue and Recovery Service (ARRS) 363, 364
AH-1 Cobra helicopter *50, 51, 213*, 216, *272-273*
AH-64 helicopter 38, *38, 39*, 50-51, *58-59*
Air assault infantry 31, 34
Air defense artillery 53
Air Force Academy 305, 306, *378-379, 379*, 380, 381, 384, *384, 385, 385,*
Air Force Communications Command (AFCC) 348, *350*
Air Force One 282, *360-361*
Air Force Reserve (AFRES) 304, 306, 375, 376
Air Force Systems Command 306, 344, 350, 353, 354, *354*, 356, *356*, 358
Air National Guard (ANG) 301, 304, 305, 308, 375, 376
Air Training Command (ATC) 375, 379, *382-383*, 383, 386
Air University 386
Airborne infantry *14, 31*, 34-35, 37
Aircraft 141-145
AirLand Battle Doctrine 11-13, 96
Alaskan Air Command (AAC) 311, 313, *318-319*, 319, 322, 348
Amphibious Assault Team 213
Amphibious Assault Vehicle (AAV) 265
Andrews AFB *360-361* , *364-365*, 365
Annapolis (see United States Naval Academy)
Apache (see AH-64)
Armor 11, 37-38
Army, Department of 25
Army National Guard 11, 22, *40*, 96
Army Reserve 11, 22, *26*, 96, *97*
AV-8 Harrier V/STOL 216, 219, 279, 280, *280*
Aviano AB *334-335*, 338, *368-369*
Aviation 38-39
Aviation Combat Element (ACE) 212, 216, 219

B-1B *296-297, 340-341*, 341
B-52 Stratofortress *340-341*, 340, 343, 344
Band (see United States Marine Band)
Basic training, Army *11, 20, 23, 31, 60*, 61-62, *61, 63, 65, 75*
Battalion Landing Team (BLT) 213

Battleships 147-155, 185
Beale AFB *300-301, 346-347*, 373
BGM 109 (GCLM) 338
Bitburg AB *336-337*
Black Hawk (see UH-60)
Blue Angels Squadron 280, *282, 284*
'Border Star 85' training exercises *26, 28, 80, 81*
Bradley Fighting Vehicles 11, *13*, 35, 38, 47, 50, *78*
Bronco (see OV-10)
Brooks AFB 308, 381
Buchli, Col James 282
Burrows, Maj William 206, 263

C-5 Galaxy *300-301, 368-369, 370-371*, 371
C-130 and KC-130 Hercules 219, 250, 260, 280, *282, 304-305*, 361, *362-363*, 363, 365, 366, *368-369*, 371, *371*, 376, *376*
C-140 Jetstar 368
C-141 *360-361, 364-365, 368-369*, 371
Camp Lejeune 252, *269*
Carr, Col Gerald P 282
Carriers 128-141, 185
Cavalry 37-38
CH-46 Sea Knight helicopter *127, 133, 181, 182-183*, 216, 274, 275, 278, *279, 287*
CH-47 helicopter *21, 41, 57*
CH-53 Sea Stallion 181, 216, 278, *278*
CH/HH-3 363, *364*
Chaparral missile system *40, 41, 41, 44, 45*, 53, *53*
Cherry Point 252
Chinook (see CH-47)
Civil War 19
Clark AB *330-331, 332-333*, 365
Cobra (see AH-1)
Combat engineers 40, 41, *41*
Combat forces, organization of 28-31
Combat Services Support Element (CSSE) 214
Combat-service support systems 57
Combat support systems 57
Combat training, Army *12-13, 15, 26, 27, 28, 34, 35, 36, 37, 42, 43, 74-75, 75, 77, 78, 81, 92, 94-95, 96*
Command Element (CE) 214
Composite Aircraft Squadron 213
Corps of Engineers 28
Criminal Investigations Command 28
Cruisers 156-160
CUCV cargo vehicle 265
Cunningham, Alfred A 274

Department of Defense 206, 302, 305, 306, 354, 358, 375
Destroyers 160-164
Direct Reporting Units (DRU) 304, 305, 306, 311
Dragon antitank missile 34

E-2C Hawkeye 143
E-3A AWACS 356
EA-6B Prowler 143, *276*
Eagle (see F-15)

Education, Army 12, 82-83
Edwards AFB 308, 356
EF-111 Raven 358, 359, 360
Eglin AFB 308, 356
Eielson AFB *320-321*, 381
Eighth Army 27, 28
82d Airborne Division 26, 85-89, *86, 88*
Electronic Security Command (ESC) 359

F-4 Phantom *135*, 141, 143, 219, 279, *290, 304-305*, 312, *313*, 322, *322, 324-325, 330-331, 332-333, 334-335*, 336, 338
F-5 Tiger 312, *315*, 336
F-14 Tomcat 109, *125, 128-129*, 141, *142*, 143, *144-145*, 188, 189
F-15 Eagle *299, 310, 311*, 312, *314-315*, 322, 325, 330, 334, 336, *336-337*, 338
F-16 Falcon *294-295, 300-301*, 312, *316-317, 318-319*, 323, 336, *338-339*
F-106 Delta Dagger 312, 375
F-111 Aardvark 312, 326, 359
F/A-18 Hornet 109, 141, 143, *143*, 219, *219*, 221, 274, 277, *279*
Falcon (see F-16)
'Fat Albert' (see C-130)
FB-111 340
Field Artillery 39-41
Fifth Army 26
Fire Support Systems 53-57
First Army 26
'Flag' exercises 317, 319
Forces Command 25-26, 28
Fourth Army 36
Frigates 164-168

Galaxy (see C-5)
Glenn, John 282
Green Berets (see Special Forces)
Grenada rescue 85-89, *86-88*, 185, 213, 243, 250, *250*, 252, *252*, 254
Ground Combat Element (GCE) 211, 212, 216
Guam *332-333*, 344

H-3 Sea King helicopter 141, 143
Harrier (see AV-8)
Hawk missile system 41, 219, *265*
Health Services Command 27
Hercules (see C-130)
HH-58 365
Hill AFB *312-313*, 353
HMMWV multipurpose vehicle 41, 265
HMX-1 282
Hohner harmonica 263
Honduras 34, 89-92, *91-93*
Hornet (see F/A-18)
Howard AFB 313, 366
Huey (see UH-1)
HUMMER (see HMMWV)
Hydrofoils 174-177

Indian Wars 15, 19
Infantry *10*, 11, 24, 31-37, *64-65, 78, 85, 94-95, 96, 97*
Information Systems Command

27
Intelligence and Security Command 27
Intruder (see A-6)
Iran 259, *259*, 260

Johnson, Opha Mae 234
'Jolly Rogers' squadron *125*

KC-10 Extender 340, 376, *386*
KC-130 (see C-130)
KC-135 Stratotanker *332-333*, 340, 358
Kelley, Paul X 206, *206*, 241, 254, 256, 282
Kelly AFB 306, 308, 353, 359
Korea, Republic of 27
Korean War 21
Kirtland AFB 306, 308
Kunsen AB *300, 323*

Lackland AFB 322, 380, 383
LAV *266-267*
Laser beam director *196*
LCAC 265
LCM *269*
Lebanon 185, *203, 211, 212, 243, 243, 244, 244, 247, 247, 248-249*, 252, *253*, 254, 270
Little Rock AFB *340-341*
Lowry AFB 306, 381, 385
Luke AFB *314-315*
LVTP-7 *250, 269*

M1 Abrams tank 11, *28*, 38, 45-58, *46*
M1A1 265
M-16 rifle *10, 21*, 34, 51, 75, *94-95*, 222, 226, *236-237*, 241, 265
M-48 *269*
M60 tank 38, 48-50, *214-215*, 265, *270*
M68 cannon 45, 58
M113 personnel carrier 38, 48-49, 50, *51*
M249 squad automatic weapon 34, 51
M939 series truck 265
Marine Aircraft Group (MAG) 216, 219
Marine Aircraft Wing (MAW) 212, 219
Marine Air Ground Task Force (MAGTF) 211, 212, 213, 216, 219
Marine Amphibious Brigade (MAB) 211, 212, 216, 265
Marine Amphibious Force (MAF) 211, 212, 219
Marine Amphibious Unit (MAU) 211, 212, 213, 216, 219, 250
Marine Aviation 274, 275, *275*, 276, 278, 280
Marine Corps One 282, *282*
Marine Pre-positioning Ships concept (MPS) 269, 270, *270*, 288
Marine Reservists 270
Marine Security Guard (MSG) 221, 256, 257, *257*, 258, 259, *259*
Materiel Command 27
Maxwell AFB 305, 381, 383, 386
Medal of Honor 287
Mexican War 15
Military Airlift Command (MAC)

336, 348, *360-361*, 361, *362-363*, 363, 364, 365, *364-365*, 366, 367, *366-367*, *368-369*, 371, 376
Military District of Washington 28
Military Traffic Management 28
Minuteman ICBM 340, 344
MK19-3 grenade launcher 34
MLRS (Multiple Launch Rocket System) 11, 41, 53-57, *54-55*
MULE 270
MV-22A Osprey 276, *276*, 278

National Command Authority 213, 219
National Training Center 13, *37*, 74-75
NASA 282, 354, 356, 358
NATO 21, 26-27, 299, *312-313*, 334, 338, *338*, 361, 383, *386-388*, 388
Naval Reserve Officers Training Corps 117
Naval training and education 117-118
Nellis AFB 308, *312-313*, 312, 317, 319, 359
NORAD 299, 313, 373
Norton AFB 306, 356, *362-363*

Officer training, Army 42-69
101st Airborne Division 26, *84*
Osan AB *322, 326-327, 327-328, 364*
Osprey (see MV-22A)
Operation *Evening Light* 259
Operation *Urgent Fury* 213, 250
OV-10 Bronco 219
Overmeyer, Col Robert F 282, *282*

Pacific Air Forces (PACAF) 311, 313, 322, 325, 326, *327-328*, 330, *332-333*, 348
Palestinian Liberation Organization (PLO) 243
Parris Island 203, *208-209*, 221
Patrick AFB 305, 353, 354
Patriot missile system 41, 53
Personnel totals, Army 22
Phantom (see F-4)
Prowler (see EA-6)

Quantico 258

Ramstein AB 301, 334, 336
Randolph AFB 306, 375, 379
Rangers *12-13*, 26, 31, *35*, 37, *74, 78, 81*, 85-87, *87*
Reagan, President Ronald 206, 244, 252, *253, 282*
Recruiting, Army 11, 22, *62*
Redeye missile launcher 219
'Reforger' training exercises *15, 16-17, 18, 19, 25*
Regimental Landing Team (RLT) 216
Revolutionary War 13, 14
RH-53D 259, 260, *260*
Rhein Main AB 336, *364-365*, 365

Scott AFB 304, 305, 306, 311, 348, 361, 364, 376
Sea Knight helicopter (see CH-46)

Sea Sparrow missile 131
Sea Stallion (see CH-53)
'Sea Whiz' (see Vulcan Phalanx)
Second Army 26
Separate Operating Agencies (SOA) 304, 305, 306, 311, 376
Sgt York gun system 53, *53*
Seventh Army 26
Seventy-fifth Infantry 85, 87
SH-60 Seahawk helicopter 164, 188
Sidewinder AAM *311*
Sixth Army 26
Shipboard organization 119-123
Skyhawk (see A-4)
Skylab 282
Sousa, John Phillip 263, *263*
Space Shuttle 282, *282*
Spanish-American War 19
Special Forces 26, 42, *42, 43*, 85
SR-71 340, *346-347*
Stinger missile system 41, 53, *53*, 219, *219*
Strategic Air Command (SAC) *332-333*, 340, 344, 348, 354, 376
Submarines 168-174
Suwon AB *320-321, 326, 376-377*

Tactical Air Command (TAC) 311, 313, 317, 334, 340, 348, 356, 365
Tactical Command, Control and Communications Systems 57
'Team Spirit' training exercises *15, 27*
Technical training, Army *82, 83, 83*
Third Army 26
Training and Doctrine Command 22, 27, 61
Tomcat (see F-14)
Travis AFB *370-371*

U-2 348
UH-1 Huey (see also VH-1) 216, *302-303, 304-305*, 363, 365
UH-60 helicopter 39, *39*, 41, *51, 56, 57, 88-89*
United States Air Force 206, 219, 250, 270, 282
United States Air Force in Europe (USAFE) 311, 313, *334-335*, 334, 336, 338, 348
United States Air Force Museum 353, *353*
United States Air Force Staff 302, 304
United States Army, 26, 27, 28, 206, 219, 250, 270, 302, 305, 306, 366, 371
United States Marine Band 263, *263*
United States Military Academy 63-69, *66-71*
United States Navy 206, 210, *216*, 219, 234, 250, 269, 270, 276, *278*, 280, 284, 299, 302, 305, 322, *364-365*, 366
United States Naval Academy 117
USS *Abraham Lincoln* 32
USS *Aguila* (PHM 4) 174
USS *America* (CV 66) *130, 143*
USS *Arkansas* (CGN 41) *162, 195-196*

USS *Bainbridge* (CGN 25) 156, 157
USS *Carl Vinson* (CVN 70) *128*, 130
USS *Cayuga* (LST 1186) *178-179, 180, 181, 290-291*
USS *Cochrane* (DDG 21) *162-163*
USS *Coral Sea* (CV 43) 132, *136-137*, 138, 141
USS *Denver* (LPD 9) *182-183*
USS *Dubuque* (LPD 8) 183
USS *Dwight D Eisenhower* (CVN 69) *130*
USS *Elliott* (DD 967) *164*
USS *Enterprise* (CVN 65) *110, 124, 132, 139, 144-145*
USS *Fife* (DD 991) *155*
USS *Fletcher* (DD 992) *160-161, 165, 166-167*
USS *George Washington* (CVN 72) 132
USS *Guam* (LPH 9) 181, 250
USS *Haleakala* (AE 25) *181*
USS *Hercules* (PHM 2) *104-105*
USS *Iowa* (BB61) 190, *122, 147*
USS *John F Kennedy* (CV 67) *128-129*
USS *Kitty Hawk* (CV 63) *134-135, 138, 187, 190-191*
USS *Knox* (FF 1052) *126*
USS *LaSalle* (AGF 3) *186*
USS *Leahy* (CG 16) *156,158-159*
USS *Long Beach* (CGN 9) 157
USS *Mars* (AFS 1) *127*
USS *Marvin Shields* (FF 1066) *160-161*
USS *McInerney* (FFG 8) *160-161*
USS *Meyercord* (FF 1058) *168*
USS *Michigan* (SSBN 727) *168-169*
USS *Midway* (CV 41) *130, 134-135, 138, 141, 187*
USS *Missouri* (BB 63) 109, *147*
USS *Mount Baker* (AE 34) *131*
USS *New Jersey* (BB 62) *102-103, 106, 108-109*, 109, *126-127, 146-147, 147, 149, 150-151, 152, 152-153, 155, 168, 184, 185*, 185, *186, 200*
USS *Nimitz* (CYN 68) *125*, 130, *131, 134-135, 138, 187, 260*
USS *Ohio* (SSBN 726) *168, 172-173*
USS *Pegasus* (PHM 1) *176-177*
USS *Peleliu* (LHA 5) *180*
USS *Portsmouth* (SSN 707) *170-171*
USS *Ranger* (CV 61) *134-135, 186*
USS *Recruit* (TDE 1) *118*
USS *Saratoga* (CV 60) 188
USS *Shreveport* (LDP 12) 186
USS *Sides* (FFG 14) *166-167*
USS *Taurus* (PHM 3) *174-175*
USS *Theodore Roosevelt* (CVN 71) 130
USS *Ticonderoga* (CG 47) *156, 160, 185*
USS *Truxton* (CGN 35) 157, *158*
USS *Underwood* (FFG 36) 164
USS *Vancouver* 269
USS *Wisconsin* (BB 64) 109, *147*

Vandenberg AFB 344, *372-373*
VC-137 282
VH-1 282 (see also UH-1)

VH-3 282
Vietnam War 21
Vulcan antiaircraft gun 50
Vulcan Phalanx Close-in Weapons System 50, 131, *146-147, 154, 155*

War of 1812 14-15
Warthog (see A-10)
Western Command *27*, 28
Western Space and Missile Test Center 354
West Point (see United States Military Academy)
'Wolfpack' squadron *144-145*
Women in the Army 20, 21-22, *72-73, 83*
Women in the Navy 117, 118
Women in the Marines 221, 226, 234, *234*, 238, 239, 241, *241*, 257, 275
World War I 19-21
World War II 21
Wright Patterson AFB 306, 353, 354, 356, 386

Yokota AB *308*

PICTURE CREDITS

bottom, 219, 254-255, 261, 264, 265, 266-267, 270, 272-273, 275 top, 276 top, 277, 279 top, 280-281 all, 284-285, 293, 294, 295, 318-319, 336-337, 339, 388

PH2 Robert Hamilton, US Navy: 112-113

MSgt Ken Hammond, USAF: 301, 303, 320-321, 322, 330-331, 330 bottom, 350 bottom, 365 top right

Sgt Dan Hardoby, US Army: 82 bottom, 83 top

TSgt Michael Harrington, USAF: 299

JOCS Kirby Harrison, US Navy: 141 bottom

TSgt Hernandez, USAF: 328-329

PH1 Jeff Hilton, US Navy: 122, 155 top

Hohner, Inc: 263

Kathleen Jaeger: 216 bottom, 282 top left

Jack Kightlinger, The White House: 206 top

Sgt Russell Kilka, USMC: 198-199, 200-201, 203, 206 second from top, 207, 208-209, 220, 221, 222 top, 223 top, 224-225, 226 both, 227 both, 228 bottom, 229 bottom, 230-231, 232, 233, 234 top, 235 both, 236-237, 238 all, 239 both, 240-241 all, 288

SMgt Buster Kellum, USAF: 306 center, 350-351, 357, 373 center, 379, 380 both, 382-383

PHC William E Kendall, US Navy: 164 bottom

Cpl Richard Kotarba, USMC: 234 bottom

LTV Aerospace and Defense Company, AM General Division: 41 top

LTV Corporation: 54-55 all.

Richard Lee, courtesy of Office, Chief Army Reserve: 10, 27 top, 32-33, 36, 81 top right, 85, 94-97 all

JO1 Lewis, US Navy: 117

TSgt Michael Longfellow, USAF: 313 top

TSgt Jose Lopez, USAF: 369 top right

PH2 David B Loveall, US Navy: 187 bottom

SSgt Marvin Lynchard, USAF, 328 top, 328 center

TSgt Bert Mau/SSgt Ron Lewis, USAF: 302 bottom

McDonnell Douglas Corporation: 58-59, 143 top, 165, 174-175

SSgt Steve McGill, USAF: 328 bottom

SSgt Donald McMichael, USAF: 364 top left

PH1 Terry C Mitchell, US Navy: 118 all, 119

NASA: 283

PHC Ron Oliver, US Navy: 121

PH3 T Olsen/PHAN M Lanway, US Navy: 132 bottom

SrA Eric Palmer, USAF: 359 bottom

SSgt Glenda Pellum, USAF: 363 bottom

SSgt Danny Perez, USAF: 298

TSgt Dennis Plummer, USAF: 305 top

TSgt Dennis Plummer/SSgt David Nolan, USAF: 376

PH2 A E Rochells, US Navy: 130 top

SSgt Lee Schading, USAF: 322, 323, 326 second from top left

PH3 Lee Schnell, US Navy: 134, 135, 187 bottom

Karl Schumacher, The White House: 282 bottom

TSgt Ernest Sealing, USAF: 362, 375 top

SSgt Fernando Serna, USAF: 309, 364 top right, 364 center, 365 top left

PH2 Rick Sforza, US Navy: 150-151, 184, 192-193

Sikorsky Aircraft Company: 51 bottom, 56, 57 second from top

©Erik Simonsen: 296-297, 310

Airman Nancy Smelser, USAF: 304

PH2 D Smith, US Navy: 155 bottom

Pete Souza, The White House: 253-254

SMSgt Don Sutherland, USAF: 313 lower right, 317 center left, 317 bottom

Perry Thorsvik, US Navy: 143 bottom

United States Air Force: 15 bottom, 18, 19 all, 25, 16 bottom, 27 bottom, 28-29, 43, 80, 81 top left, 213 bottom, 302 top and center, 304-305, 308, 311, 315, 316, 317 top, 319 top, 324, 325 bottom, 326 top, 327, 331 top, 331 bottom left and right, 334-335, 338, 340 bottom, 341, 343 second from top, 343 bottom, 348-349, 348 bottom, 349 top, 349 bottom, 350 top, 352, 356, 358 top, 360 top, 363 top, 366 top both, 368 top left, 374-375

United States Air Force Academy: 378, 384-385 all four

United States Department of Defense: 8-9, 11, 14 bottom, 16-17, 34 all, 40 top, 41 bottom, 46-47, 48-49 all, 50 top, 51 top, 61, 63 both, 74 top, 75 top, 82 top, 83 middle right, 84, 86-87 all, 88-89 all, 90-91, 92-93 all, 127 right,

158-159, 162-163, 169, 183 top, 199, 202, 210 top, 212 top, 243, 244 both, 245, 246 top and inset, 247 both, 248-249, 250-251 all, 252 both, 253 top left and right

United States Marine Corps: 210 bottom, 212 bottom, 217 top left and right, 218 top three, 222 middle and bottom, 223 bottom left and right, 228 top, 229 top, 242, 246 bottom, 256-257 both, 258 top, 262, 263 top three, 274 bottom, 278 bottom, 286

United States Navy: 107, 111, 125, 126-127, 128 left, 130-131, 135 both, 138 both, 140, 141 top, 142, 144-145, 156 left, 156-157, 158 top, 162 top, 164 top, 168 both, 173 top, 181 bottom, 188 bottom, 216 top, 258-259 bottom, 259 top, 260 both, 268, 269 both, 270-271, 272 all, 274-275, 275 bottom, 278 top, 287 all

TSgt Kurt Vall, USAF: 330 top

Walt Weible, USAF: 354-355, 372, 381

W M Welch, US Navy: 130 bottom

Bob Williams, USAF: 314

PH1 Wood, US Navy: 116

©Bill Yenne: 102-103, 106, 108-109, 110, 114-115, 123, 124, 136-137, 146-147, 147, 148, 149, 154, 154-155, 160-161, 166-167, 178-179, 180, 181 top, 182-183, 185, 186 bottom, 190-191, 194-195, 197, 279 bottom, 282 top right, 290-291, 300-301, 340 top, 342-343, 344-345, 353, 359 top, 360-361, 364-365, 365 top, 368-369, 369 top, 373 top, 386-387.